THE TIMES TWO BRAINS

D & B Publishing

New and forthcoming books.

D & B Poker

1-904468-06-3	*Poker on the Internet*	Andrew Kinsman
1-904468-08-X	*How Good is your Pot-Limit Hold'em?*	Stewart Reuben
1-904468-07-1	*How Good is your Pot-Limit Omaha?*	Stewart Reuben

D & B Bridge

1-904468-09-8	*Defensive Plays*	Sally Brock
1-904468-00-4	*No Trump Contracts*	David Bird
1-904468-01-2	*Suit Contracts*	Brian Senior

D & B Puzzles

1-904468-02-0	*400 IQ Puzzles*	Carter and Russell
1-904468-10-1	*Solving IQ Puzzles*	Carter and Russell
1-904468-11-X	*Solving Word Puzzles*	Carter and Russell
1-904468-03-9	*200 Word Puzzles*	Carter and Russell

D & B General

1-904468-13-6	*Online Gambling*	Angus Dunnington

D & B Publishing, PO Box 18, Hassocks, West Sussex BN6 9WR, UK
Tel: 01273 834680, Fax: 01273 831629, e-mail: info@dandbpublishing.com,
Website: www.dandbpublishing.com

THE TIMES

IQ, word and logic puzzles, as published in The London Times

two brains

Ray Keene & Byron Jacobs

Viva Books Private Limited

New Delhi • Mumbai • Chennai • Kolkata • Hyderabad • Bangalore

First Indian Edition 2005

VIVA BOOKS PRIVATE LIMITED

- 4262/3 Ansari Road, Daryaganj, New Delhi 110 002
  E-mail: viva@vivagroupindia.net
- 215-216 New Apollo Estate, 2nd Floor, Mogra Lane, Andheri (E), Mumbai 400 069
  E-mail: vivamumbai@vivagroupindia.net
- Jamals Fazal Chambers, 26 Greams Road, Chennai 600 006
  E-mail: vivachennai@vivagroupindia.net
- B-103, Jindal Towers, 21/1A/3, Darga Road, Kolkata-700 017
  E-mail: vivakolkata@vivagroupindia.net
- 7 GF, Sovereign Park Apts., 56-58 K. R. Road, Basavanagudi, Bangalore 560 004
  Email: vivabangalore@vivagroupindia.net
- 101 & 102, Mughal Marc Apartments, Narayanaguda, Hyderabad 500 029
  E-mail: vivahyderabad@vivagroupindia.net

Published by arrangement with

D & B Publishing
P.O Box 18, Hassocks
West Sussex BN6 9WR,
UK

ISBN 81-7649-949-8

Published by Vinod Vasishtha for Viva Books Private Limited, 4262/3 Ansari Road, New Delhi 110 002 and printed and bound at Sanat Printers, Kundli - 131028.

CONTENTS

INTRODUCTION

The Times Two Brains column is published once a week and features numerous brain teasers, which are often submitted by readers. Over the past few years, many fascinating puzzles have been published in the column and a substantial forum has developed with people writing in to claim that answers given are controversial or to point out possible alternative solutions. The email address associated with the column regularly receives around 50 emails per week as well as numerous communications by post.

Of all the puzzles that have been published in the last five years, the one which has been responsible for the largest postbag is the following:

> You are in a quiz show with a chance to win a million pounds by selecting the correct box from three. The host – and this is *very* important – knows which box contains the million. You make your choice and then the host opens one of the other boxes to reveal it as empty. He then offers you the chance to change your mind and select the remaining box. Should you do this?

You may wish to consider the problem yourself before looking up the solution. The problem is number 197 in the book and the answer is given on page 134.

This question generated an extraordinary postbag with over 100 people writing in or emailing, almost all claiming that the answer given was nonsense. Some of these included professional mathematicians. However, this is not the first time that this question has elicited such a response. In the book *Taking Chances* written by John Haigh (Oxford

University Press), the author recounts how Marilyn vos Savant, said to have the highest IQ in the world, gave a correct explanation of this puzzle to the readers of her 'Ask Marilyn' column in *Parade* Magazine. The reaction was more or less the same. As Haigh writes: 'Her postbag bulged with excited letters, some from professors in university statistics departments, asserting that she was wrong'.

This puzzle also bamboozled the Hungarian Paul Erdos, who was one of the most brilliant and successful mathematicians of the 20th century. In his biography of Erdos (*The Man Who Loved only Numbers*, 4th Estate) Paul Hoffman relates how Erdos was given the problem by his colleague Andrew Vazsonyi and got the answer wrong. When he was told the correct answer and given the explanation, he simply refused to believe it. He walked away and eventually began to get quite agitated about it. As Hoffman writes: 'Vazsonyi had seen this reaction before, in his students, but he hardly expected it from the most prolific mathematician of the 20th century.'

This goes to show the incredible fascination that brainteasers and puzzles in logic can generate. We hope you enjoy this collection of the best of the problems published in *The Times*.

Raymond Keene and Byron Jacobs
May 2003.

two brains

QUESTIONS 1-100

Question 1 — COASTAL WATERS

Land is to sea as .... is to strait?

Question 2 — THREE BY FOUR

Insert the missing number:

2	4	8	4
6	5	3	10
4	3	?	8

Question 3 — THREES

Insert the missing number:

16		11
	9	
25		14
	13	
16		5
	?	

Question 4 — MISSING NUMBER

What is the missing number?

6, 7, 9, 8, ?, 8, 6

Question 5 — SEX

Tri is to sex as quad is to ....?

Question 6 — SEQUENCE #1

What is the next number in this sequence?

4, 19, 49, 109, ???

Question 7 — SEQUENCE #2

What is the next number in this sequence?

4, 5, 8, 17, 44, ???

Question 8 — SEQUENCE #3

What is the next number in this sequence?

4, 4, 5, 13, 40, ???

Question 9 — WHOSE NEXT?

Who comes next?

Harold, James, Michael, Neil, John, ???

Question 10 BOGUS WORDS

Which of the following words are bogus?
Atoks, Cruve, Emf, Nauplii, Plongs, Woktu.

Question 11 GREEK ALPHABET

Ten letters have been randomly allocated different values from 0 to 9. The sum of the letter values in GAMMA is 30, in ETA is 11, THETA 23, IOTA 20, PI 12 and PHI 20. What are the values of ALPHA and OMEGA?

Question 12 CAT SUMS

In the following sum each of the digits from 0 to 9 is used. Given that S+V=E, can you make the sum work?

```
    A
  CAT
  HAS
 NINE
-----
LIVES
```

BRAIN FLASH: Research suggests that stimulating the mind with mental exercise may cause brain cells to branch wildly. This branching causes millions of additional connections. 'Think of it as a computer with a bigger memory board. You can do more things more quickly' (Arnold Scheibel, Director of Brain Research Institute, UCLA).

Question 13 HEATING

When you place a pan of water on the cooker, what method transfers the heat to the water?

Radiation, Conduction, Thermal, Convection, Molecular

Question 14 MYTHICAL QUANTITIES

Match the following names and numbers:

Polyphemus, Sleipnir, Briareos, Shelob, The Kraken

100, 8, 1, 10, 8

Question 15 SEQUENCE #4

What is the next number in this sequence?

3, 4, 6, 12, 36, ?

Question 16 PROFESSIONS

The two statements below can be read as two professions. What are they?

a) GO NURSE
b) MOON STARER

Question 17 A TO F

What numbers can replace these letters?
ABCDEF x 3 = BCDEFA

Question 18 — SERIES #1

Which letter is next in this series?

O T T F F S S

Question 19 — TOP CAT

If DG = 53 and FT = 406, what does TC equal?

Question 20 — VOWELLED

Name two five letter words which use four different vowels plus the letter 'd'?

Question 21 — ADDITION

What numbers can replace these letters? (No zero or 3)

```
  ABC
+ BDG
----
 EFGB
```

BRAIN FLASH: Verbal intelligence is one of the major factors in IQ testing. Vocabulary has been found to be the single type of intelligence most highly correlated with success. Numerical intelligence is the second major factor in IQ testing and refers to the ability to play with the numerical alphabet.

Question 22 ANIMAL

What animal can be formed by using all of these letters?

a, e, m, m, o, r, s, t

Question 23 DAYS

If FRIDAY = 63 and SUNDAY = 84, what day = 100?

Question 24 NAMES

Can you think of people's names which answer these clues?

a) Highly coloured variety of quartz?
b) Evergreen: emblem of love?
c) Plant of the mint family?
d) French gold coin?

Question 25 GREETINGS

Why is this a Christmas greeting?

ABCDEFGHIJKMNOPQRSTUVWXYZ

Question 26 SUBSTANCE

What substance is denoted here?

HIJKLMNO

Question 27 — CENSUS

A census taker comes to a house and asks how many people live there. He is told there are three. Then he asks what their ages are and is told that the product of the three ages is 200 and the sum of the three ages is the number of the house. The census taker then thinks a while and says: 'I cannot figure out the ages from this information. I must ask another question: is there someone in the house over 21?' The answer is yes and now the census taker knows the three ages. What are they?

Question 28 — GAGGLE

Gaggle is to Geese as Pod is to ....?

Question 29 — CRYPTOLOGY

If
ENGLAND = 4623165
LEG = 453
DANGLE = 738456

what does AND equal?

Question 30 — PRIDE

Pride is to Lions as .... is to Crows?

Question 31 — SQUARE ROOTS

What are the two square roots of 28355625?

Question 32 DOUBLE MEANING

Party (............) Sphere

What missing word has the same meaning as the two outer words?

Question 33 FIENDS

Which Shakespearean character called whom 'juggling fiends'?

Question 34 JUGGLING

A man weighing 140 pounds wishes to cross a bridge that will take a maximum weight of 150 pounds but will collapse if this is exceeded, even minutely. He has three identical objects, each weighing 5 pounds. Since one object will always be in the air, can safely cross the bridge by juggling?

Question 35 SEQUENCE #5

Take the following sequence:

8, ?, 4, ?, 1, ?, 6, ?, 2

Insert the missing digits (i.e. 3, 5, 7 and 9 – not 0) in such a way that the resulting sequence is in a simple and logical order.

Question 36 SWITCHES

There are three electric switches on the outside of a sealed room and each works a lamp inside. You can turn the switches on or off as you like but you are allowed to look inside or go inside the room only once. How can you decide which switch works which lamp?

Question 37 CAPITALISE

If FDB + CEG = III, what is missing from the following sum?

EHA + ??? = III

(note: the answer to both sums consists of three capital 'I's, not ones)

Question 38 GROUPS

Which other letter of the alphabet will belong with the following group?

B, C, D, E, G, P, T

Question 39 MIXTURES

If R + Y = O and B + R = P, what does Y + B = ?

Question 40 SEQUENCE #6

What number is missing from this sequence?

4, 7, ?, 18, 29, 47

BRAIN FLASH: The brain weighs about the same as a bag of sugar – approximately 2% of bodyweight. But it accounts for up to 20% of the bodies energy needs. Each nerve cell in the brain can be connected with up to 100,000 others. Counting each nerve connection in the human brain cortex – the outer layer – at the rate of one per second would take 32 million years.

Question 41 — SEVEN LETTERS

Complete the following sentence with two different seven letter words. The words used must be anagrams, i.e. the same seven letters must be used for both words.

He has been her ? on ? occasions.

Question 42 — CITY NUMBERS

If OXFORD = 60, YORK = 275 and INVERNESS = 171, what does MANCHESTER = ?

Question 43 — PALINDROMES

Which of these words does not belong with the others?

CIVIC, FEWER, RADAR, LEVEL and REFER

Question 44 — BILL

In a restaurant a man orders a meal and a drink. The bill comes to £11. If the meal costs £10 more than the drink, how much does the drink cost?

Question 45 — CONNECTIONS

'Time's running past' we murmur, is an anagram of four words connected to each other and the sentence. What are the words?

Question 46 — AGES

If CHARLES is 50, SYLVESTER is 45 and KEVIN is 4, how old is LOUISE?

Question 47 — SERIES #2

What letter should come next in this series?

J, F, M, A, M, ?

Question 48 — SWEETS

If Sam gives Chloe three sweets they will both have the same number of sweets. If Chloe gives Sam three sweets Sam will have four times as many sweets as Chloe. Who has what?

Question 49 — DEAD POETS

At the Annual General Meeting of the Dead Poets Society a steward mixed up the letters of some of the delegates' names. Can you help out by giving the correct names?

TOILETS, NERDDY, TOMNIL, EASESHEPARK

Question 50 — QUOTATION #1

One of the above wrote the following. Can you identify it?

'They say there's but five upon this isle: we are three of them; if the other two be brain'd like us the state totters.'

Question 51 CHRONOLOGY

Place the following in chronological order from most recent to most distant.

CRISTIAS, BROCANISEFOUR, SUJARCIS, TRACESOUCE

Question 52 QUOTATION #2

Can you identify the following quotation?

'What the hammer? What the chain?
In what furnace was thy brain?'

Question 53 QUOTATION #3

Can you identify the following quotation?

'... a false creation,
Proceeding from the heat oppressed brain'

Question 54 TRIANGLES

Find the missing number:

35 37 13 5 3
36 25 9 ??

BRAIN FLASH: A million million nerve cells are packed into every human head. There are as many cells between your ears as there are stars in the Milky Way galaxy.

Question 55 PLANETS

If earth = 1, match the following names and numbers.

Neptune, Uranus, Saturn, Jupiter

18, 8, 16, 15

Question 56 MORE PLANETS

If earth = 1, match the following names and numbers.

Pluto, Mars, Venus, Mercury

0.2408, 0.6152, 1.881, 248.5

Question 57 ELEMENTARY

Match these substances with these numbers.

Hydrogen, Helium, Lithium, Carbon, Oxygen

6, 2, 8, 3, 1

Question 58 SATELLITES

Match the following names from the first list with those in the second.

Mars, Jupiter, Saturn, Uranus, Neptune, Pluto

Charon, Titan, Miranda, Io, Triton, Phobos

Question 59 CAST LIST

What word connects the film roles of Professor Higgins, Dr Dolittle, Han Solo and Indiana Jones?

Question 60 BEAR

Can you identify the following quotation and who said it?

'I am a Bear of Very Little Brain, and long words Bother me.'

Question 61 BRAIN WEIGHT

What is the approximate weight of the average human brain?

Question 62 QUOTATION #4

Who said the following and where?

'In my youth,' Father William replied to his son,
'I feared it might injure the brain;
But now that I'm perfectly sure I have none,
Why, I do it again and again.'

Question 63 CONNECTIONS

What is the potential number of connections for one brain cell?

10^5, 10^{15}, 10^{28}, 10^{47}

Question 64	BRAIN CELL

What do we call a brain cell: synapse, axon, dendrite or neuron?

Question 65	QUOTATION #5

'A man should his keep his little brain attic stocked with all the furniture that he is likely to use, and the rest he can put away in the lumber-room of his library.' What is the source?

Question 66	SEQUENCE #7

What is the next number in this sequence?

VII, V, VIII, VI, ??

Question 67	MUDDLE

At the annual Conference of the Brain Users Association, the signs for the lectures on cinematography, geology, classical Greek statues and osteology became jumbled. Can you help sort them out?

BRAIN FOFILE, MAC BRAIN, ELMSLEG BRAIN, MUMU BRAIN

Question 68	KNIGHT MOVES

What is the product of the shortest numbers of moves for a chess knight to travel from the square b1 to reach h8 and the shortest number of moves for a knight to reach b6 from g1?

Question 69 SUBSTANCES

Can you now match these substances with these numbers?

Hydrogen, Carbon, Nitrogen, Oxygen, Helium

14, 16, 12, 4, 1

Question 70 QUOTATION #6

Who said and where?

'The brain of this foolish-compounded clay, man, is not able to invent anything that tends to laughter, more than I invent, or is invented on me: I am not only witty in myself, but the cause that wit is in other men.'

Question 71 QUOTATION #7

Who wrote and where?

'The petrifactions of a plodding brain'

Question 72 COSMIC SUMS

If (Venus + Earth) x Neptune = 40, how much is (Jupiter – Mercury) x Pluto?

Question 73 QUOTATION #8

Who said?

'Memory – the warder of the brain'.

Question 74 FAMILY SUMS

If (Henry x Edward) – William = 60, how much is (Richard + Stephen) x Charles?

Question 75 ANOTHER MUDDLE

Those brain users are still at it. At the Braintree Local Association meeting they once again muddled up the signs for their lecture topics. Can you help?

African studies, Middle Eastern studies, Modern cartoon techniques and Latin American studies.

OI BRAIN, AH BRAIN, ADL BRAIN, USE BRAIN SOE

Question 76 DIGITAL DEDUCTION

Number A is of indeterminate length but ends in 4. Number B has the same number of digits as A, starts with 4 and is 4 times the size of A. Using this information alone, can you work out both numbers?

BRAIN FLASH: 'The experts tell you that, as you get older, your brain shrinks and you can't memorise so much. But it's actually the reverse. If you compare my results with 1993, the amount of information that I memorised this year has doubled since then, even though my brain is supposedly shrinking. So it's simply not true. It's a case of – if you don't use it, you lose it. The answer is: exercise your brain daily as I do, and it will get stronger.' World Memory Champion Dominic O'Brien, after his successful 1997 defence of his title.

Question 77 GENERALS

Can you match the following?

Wellington, Cardigan, Caesar, Kutuzov, Marlborough

Borodino, Blenheim, Waterloo, Balaklava, Alesia

Question 78 ZERO HOUR

In a pitch battle at dead of night a strategically important bridge will be blown up in 40 minutes. Four soldiers must cross to the other side in safety but only two can travel at any given moment and their is only one lamp between them. Soldier A takes one minute to cross, soldier B five minutes, soldier C fifteen minutes and soldier D twenty. What is the optimum sequence for crossing the bridge?

Question 79 THEORISTS

Can you complete the following?

Marx is to Communism as Darwin is to ....?
Einstein is to relativity as Cuvier is to ....?
Nelson is to Victory as Columbus is to ....?
Kirk is to Enterprise as Jason is to ....?

Question 80 ROYAL MEANS

If the average of Victoria, Elizabeth I and Mary I is 1649, what is the average of John, George I and William I?

Question 81 NAME LINKS

Which name links the following?

Groan
Oates
Andronicus
Flavius Sabinus Vespasianus?

Question 82 QUEENS

How many queens can be placed on an open chessboard of 64 squares without any threatening any other – what are the optimal squares?

Question 83 PERRY

Distinguish between the following:

Frederick John Perry, Matthew Perry, Perry Mason, Perry White, The Peer and the Peri.

Question 84 MIDDLE AGES

The product of the ages of three ex-teenagers is 17710. Find their ages.

Question 85 ADMIRALS

Link the following:

Howard, Nelson, Don John, Themistocles, Howe.
Aboukir, Salamis, The Armada, Ushant, Lepanto.

Question 86 SEQUENCE #8

Look at the following sequence of numbers:

2, 3, ?, 7, 11, 13, ?, 19.

Firstly, fill in the gaps, and then calculate the product of the entire sequence. For genius credit do not use a calculator or pen and paper.

Question 87 DIETS

Dietary habits. Lion is to wildebeest as giraffe is to ....?

Question 88 HANDKERCHIEFS

During a total electricity blackout you are picking handkerchiefs and wish to make sure that you have at least two of one colour. The choices are yellow, pink, white, brown and blue. How many handkerchiefs do you need to pick, sight unseen?

Question 89 INSIDE

What is the word inside this circle?

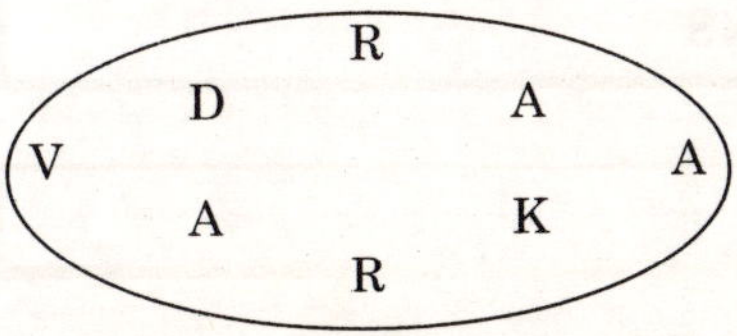

Question 90 ATHLETES

Athlete 4 always beats Athlete 1, while Athlete 2 beats 3, but loses to 1. Who finishes last?

Question 91 SEQUENCE #9

What are the next two numbers in this sequence?

6, 12, 24, 30, 60, 66, 132, ??, ??

Question 92 ZAMA

Hannibal is to Zama as Napoleon is to ....?

Question 93 SEQUENCE #10

What are the next two numbers in this sequence?

97, 106, 99, 108, 101, 110, 103, ??, ??

Question 94 ADAM

In what respect should an illustration of the Biblical Adam differ anatomically from any other man?

Question 95 SIMULTANEOUS EQUATIONS

(X-4)/8 = Y
(X+6)/10 = Y
What is X?

BRAIN FLASH: In 1994, Tathagat Avtar Tulsi from Delhi, when aged six, calculated the value of pi to seven decimal places (3.1415927).

Question 96 WINDOW SHOPPING

Window shopping in New York you realise that buying item A plus item B costs you $110. Buying item A plus item C costs you $98, while buying item C plus item B costs $114. You only have one British fifty pound note in your purse but you can change it into dollars at the rate of one pound for 1.6 dollars. You want to get the most expensive item. Which is it, how much does each item costs in dollars and how many dollars change do you get?

Question 97 TRUTH AND LIES

John always lies – Jim always tells the truth. One said: 'The other one says he is John.' Who said this?

Question 98 HUNGRY TORTOISE

A tortoise is heading for a tasty piece of fresh lettuce at the other end of the garden. The garden is 6 metres long and the tortoise moves at the rate of 1 metre an hour. However, after each hour's advance, the tortoise instantly falls asleep and a naughty boy immediately moves it back half a metre. This at once wakes the tortoise, which proceeds with its advance. How long does it take the tortoise to reach the lettuce?

Question 99 RACE

In a five way race A came before B but after C. D came before E but after B. What was the final line up?

Question 100 THREE BEARS

The three bears were having a picnic at a round table in the forest. One ate honey, another berries and the third nuts. Papa bear sat on the right of the berry eater, while mama bear sat to the right of baby bear. Who was eating the berries?

two brains

QUESTIONS 101-200

Question 101 HOW OLD?

'A' is twice as old as 'B' was when 'A' was as old as 'B' is now. If 'B' is 24, how old is 'A'?

Question 102 CHESS SETS

I recently sold four chess sets for a total of £1600. The Staunton set went for the same as the Barleycorn and half the Lewis. The barleycorn sold for the price of the Russian set minus the price of the Lewis. The Lewis was a third of the Staunton. The Russian set equalled the total of the barleycorn and the Lewis. How much was each set?

Question 103 HOOVERED

The concierge took out half the money hidden in her mattress to buy herself a new vacuum cleaner. Unfortunately, when her wages were late she had to sell it at a loss two months later, receiving back only 75% of the price she had paid. When she stuffed the money back into her mattress she had 300 Francs less than she started with. How much did the vacuum cleaner cost?

Question 104 ON EXPENSES

Three businessmen decided to divide their dinner cost equally, even though they had not consumed items of the same price. The chairman paid an extra £15. The Vice President paid £21 less than he should, while the CEO, who should have paid £165, had to fork out £6 more. What was the total bill and what should the other two have paid?

BRAIN FLASH: The highest ever prize for a Mind Sports event was the $5 million shared by chess champions Bobby Fischer and Boris Spassky for their rematch in 1992.

Question 105 EXPANDING SPACE

A connoisseur of expensive chess sets needed to enlarge the space in his den to increase his collection. He made the display space larger by 50% thus creating room for all the sets he owned plus two more. If each set takes up one square foot of space, how many chess sets does he now own?

Question 106 CHARITY BALL

At the charity ball, members paid £57.50, while guests paid £95.00. The sum of £36,250.00 was raised and 50% more members than guests attended. How many members and how many guests were there?

Question 107 ARMY WIVES

General 'A', Colonel 'B' and Major 'C' dined with their wives at a circular table. Husbands and wives alternated but no officer sat next to his wife. If the colonel was two to the right of the major and the colonel's wife two to the right of the major's wife, who sat on the general's right?

Question 108 GRANNY SMITH

Granny Smith, who was born in a leap year, was very superstitious about her shopping and always insisted on odd numbers of the items she had purchased in her shopping bags. She also felt uncomfortable when she came home after a shopping trip with an empty bag, and she absolutely refused to have just one item in a bag. One day, having left home with four bags she discovered that she had spent all her cash and acquired exactly 11 apples. How did she ensure that she had an odd number of apples in each bag and that no bag was empty or contained just one apple?

Question 109 MONOPOLY

I bought a deluxe Monopoly set but lost a playing piece on the way home and had to go back to the shop for a replacement. Together, the set and the extra piece cost £101.00. The set cost £100.00 more than the replacement piece. What did each cost?

Question 110 FAMILY GODS

Relationships in Norse mythology between Gods, their pets and mortals were very complicated and many legends grew up around them. One legend had it that Odin's eight-legged horse Sleipnir was the product of the union between Odin himself (disguised as a stallion) and fellow God Loki (in the shape of a mare). Another myth has it that Brunnhilde the Valkyrie was Odin's daughter by the earth Goddess, while a third states that Odin was also the father of the mortals Sigmund and Sieglinde, who were brother and sister. The hero Siegfried was the son of this pair and he became betrothed (accidentally) to the Rhine Princess Gutrune. If Siegfried and Gutrune had had a child, what would its relationship have been with

a) Brunnhilde?
b) Odin's magic horse?

Question 111 WAGNER

To what question might Richard Wagner have reasonably responded '9W!'?

Question 112 BEAM ME UP

On a diplomatic mission the Starship Enterprise cruised at sub-warp speed between the planet Vulcan and its furthest moon, at 50,000 kilometres per hour. On the return trip it travelled at 75,000 kph. As the trip was slowed down by a meteor shower, it took the Enterprise two hours longer to do the outward journey than the return. How far apart are Vulcan and its moon?

Question 113 — CHICKEN OR BEEF?

In the sanatorium three inmates, Adolf, Albert and Josef, developed a fixed dining pattern. Each evening the choice was restricted to either chicken or beef. If Adolf has chicken, Albert has beef. Either Adolf or Josef order chicken but not both. Albert and Josef do not both have beef. Which of the three had chicken one day and beef the next?

Question 114 — MONSTER MASH

At the conference on archetypes in literature and myth one lecturer mixed up the notes. Can you correctly associate the following characters with the appropriate monster?

Bilbo Baggins – The Giant Squid
Frodo Baggins – The Lernean Hydra
Hercules – Grendel
Captain Nemo – Smaug the Dragon
Beowulf – Shelob the Spider

Question 115 — SEQUENTIAL SUMS

After answering the following three questions, add 'a' to 'c' then subtract 'b'.

a)	14	17	20	??
b)	93	85	77	??
c)	1	12	12	
	3	4	12	
	10	20	??	

Question 116 — A DAY AT THE RACES

Can you work out this mix up and assign the right horse to each real or fictional character?

Wellington – Pegasus
Alexander the Great – Incitatus
Caligula – Copenhagen
Odin – Bucephalus
Perseus – Sleipnir

Question 117 — SMART SUMS

Puzzle 'a' has two possible solutions. Add them together and then multiply the result by the answer from 'b'.

a) 6, 11, 28, ??
   12, 22, 14, 6
b) I N T 5 L L I ? 5 N C 5

Question 118 — GEOGRAPHY

Some inattentive schoolchildren have given imaginative answers to the question as to which object belongs where. Can you sort them out?

Saqqara – Temple of Zeus
Rhodes – The Parthenon
Athens – The Step Pyramid
Moscow – The Lincoln Memorial
Washington – The Kremlin
Olympia – The Colossus

Question 119 MORE SEQUENTIAL SUMS

Deduct missing number 'b' from 'a'.

a) 1, 4, 9, 61, 52, 63, 94, ??
b) 9, 11, 21, 23, 33, 35, ??

Question 120 COMMANDERS

Whose name is indelibly associated with which battle, either as winner or loser?

Rameses II – Teutoberger Forest
Antony and Cleopatra – Kadesh
Hermann – Actium
Leonidas – The Wilderness
Ulysses S Grant – Thermopylae

Question 121 MISSING VOWELS

All the vowels have been removed from the following well known saying. Can you reconstruct it?

FLND HSMN YRSN PRTD

BRAIN FLASH: Readers of *The Washington Post* voted for Genghis Khan as Man of the Millennium. Other category winners were:

Biggest Mistake: Invading Russia.
Greatest Invention: the printing press.
Greatest Painting: Michelangelo's Sistine Chapel ceiling.
Greatest Scientist: Albert Einstein.
Greatest Genius: Shakespeare.
Greatest Musical Composition: Mozart's *The Marriage of Figaro*.

Question 122 — 12 DAYS OF CHRISTMAS

On the first day of Christmas my True Love sent to me a Partridge in a Pear Tree. The plan was to continue according to tradition over the 12 days of Christmas with Turtle Doves, French Hens, Calling Birds, Gold Rings, Geese-a-Laying, Swans-a-Swimming, Maids-a-Milking, Ladies Dancing, Lords-a-Leaping, Pipers Piping and Drummers Drumming. However things did not go to plan.

50% of the Partridges were diverted to a top London restaurant and devoured; one third of the French Hens were held up at Calais by EEC red tape; 25% of the Gold Rings were snatched by magpies and 35% of the Swans-a-Swimming were being auditioned by Sir David Attenborough. To make matters worse, five Maids-a-Milking eloped with the same number of drummers drumming, six of the ladies dancing defected from the Royal Ballet to form a new company and were too busy rehearsing to come, and 90% of the Lords-a-Leaping were hereditary peers and lost their seats, so refused to co-operate in protest.

If all had gone according to plan how many gifts would have been received?

Question 123 — PRESENTS

Following on from Question 122 – and how many did I actually get?

BRAIN FLASH: Zerah Colburn was born in Vermont, USA in 1840 and at the age of eight demonstrated a remarkable ability for the mental multiplication of powers. At London in 1848 Zerah raised 8 to the 16th power, the answer being: 241,474,976,710,656. Meanwhile as a further tremendous demonstration of mental powers, Mirat Arikan (born 1973) calculated the 39th root of an arbitrarily chosen 100 digit number in just 39 seconds. This took place in Istanbul, Turkey in 1996.

Question 124 WINTER FUEL

Winter fuel in Bohemia is subject to market forces, but is – with rare exceptions – inflationary. On Christmas Eve a single log costs 4 groats, while a bundle of 5 logs attracts a 10% discount. There are 100 pfennigs to the groat, the pfennig being the smallest unit of currency and in all calculations any fractions of pfennigs are simply eliminated.

On Christmas Day, the price of both logs and bundles increase by 2%. On Boxing Day the price increases by a further 5% on the new level, while on December 27 the price of both items escalates by a further 10%. Up to and including New Year's Day, the price increases over the previous day's level by a steady 2% each day. However, on January 2 a large shipment of logs arrives from the neighbouring province of Ruritania and the price goes into reverse. Compared with January 1, prices of individual logs fall by 50% while bundles now attract a 15% discount.

On January 2, what is the combined cost of three bundles and two logs?

Question 125 MORE WINTER FUEL

And what would four logs have cost on December 30?

Question 126 LIFE ON MARS?

Starfleet is mobilising for its new year programme of space exploration and Admiral Kirk has ordered a number of important solar system initiatives involving your section.

You are told to search for sentient life forms on the following moons in ascending order of their mean distance from the sun: Charon, Titania, Phobos, Triton and Io. Which sequence should you follow?

Question 127 MISSION

On your return Admiral Kirk then sends you on a voyage to hunt for life forms on the moons of Venus and Mercury. What conclusion do you draw from this?

Question 128 MILITARY MATHS

If Waterloo multiplied by Trafalgar = 3276075, then what are:

a) Marston Moor multiplied by Naseby?
b) Hastings plus Agincourt?

Question 129 LEGENDARY

Professor Dodecahedron of the Peloponnese School of Classical Myth has confused his lecture notes on numerology in Greek and Roman legends, and a bright graduate student has had to disentangle his topics from his numbers. Can you do as well?

The three labours of Hercules
The Twelve Muses
The twenty-four Graces
The nine Books of Homer's Iliad.

Question 130 FIGHTER PLANES

A Stakhanovite worker in a 1930s Moscow aircraft factory singlehandedly constructed 25 fighter planes in just five weeks, each week constructing 1.5 more aircraft than during the preceding week. What quantity of fighter planes did he put together during his week of activity?

Question 131 MILKMAIDS

If 6 milkmaids can fill 6 pails of milk in just 6 minutes, how many milkmaids does it take to fill 100 pails in 100 minutes?

Question 132 STRIPES

On the annual migration of the million-strong herds in the Serengeti plain 80% had stripes on their bodies, 650,000 had a black stripe between their horns, 950,000 had striped legs and 750,000 had striped tails. What is the minimum number of animals that were striped in all four areas?

Question 133 KNOCKOUT CHESS

In the year 2000, The British Chess Federation decides to re-organise its national championship into a 32 player knockout system. How many matches are required between individual players before a winner emerges?

Question 134 ENGLISH LIT

Professor Polonius of the maths department and Dr Mephistopheles of the English Literature facility of Wittenberg University have combined forces to investigate arcane numerology in the English Classics. Can you help them with two gaps in their text?

What is the product of the two missing numbers in the following quotations?

a) 'The ??? natural shocks the flesh is heir to.'
b) 'Was this the face that launched ??? ships and burnt the topless towers of Ilium?'

Question 135 PRINTS

Wittenberg Museum owns a fine collection of Oriental prints plus one fragment. The decision has been taken by Herr Director Cornelius to catalogue their possessions. Of the total number of prints, 350 are Indian, 160 are Chinese and 45% Japanese. What is the smallest possible total number of full prints in the collection?

Question 136 NUMEROLOGY

Professor Polonius and Dr Mephistopheles are still investigating numerology in the English Classics. Now, though, their team has been strengthened by the addition of Senior Lecturer Lutwidge and Vice Chancellor Alfred. Can you help them with two further gaps? What numbers do you get when you add the two missing numbers in the following quotations?

a) 'Into the valley of death rode the ???'
b) 'Sometimes I've believed as many as ??? impossible things before breakfast'

Question 137 EPIC QUEST

During Sir Galahad's epic quest for the Holy Grail he finally arrived at the Bridge of Doom guarded by a ghastly minion of Morgan le Fay. The Guardian would only let him cross the bridge if the knight could correctly answer the following question – 'Will I let you pass?' What should Sir Galahad say to get across?

Question 138 CRYPTIC CONNECTION

Why does the sequence HIJKLMNO connect the following missing letters?

The Slough of Des????
Sir Percy B????ney
A ??? of troubles

Question 139 GONE FISHING

After a severe storm in the prime fishing grounds Captain Haddocks' weekly trawling expedition – which normally lasts 15 hours – netted 6/10ths less Dover sole than he was used to catching on one excursion. Presuming the proportion of Dover sole stayed at this level for the rest of the week, how much longer would he need to go fishing during that week to catch his normal quote of Dover sole?

Question 140 BEAR HUNT

Hubert the Hunter is tracking a bear which is 100 yards due North of him. Hubert moves 100 yards due east from his original position while the bear stays put. Hubert now fires due North from his new position and hits the bear. What colour is the bear?

Question 141 HUNTER

Hubert sets off at 4.00pm to walk to his igloo to fetch a sledge to bring back the bear. Walking at 3 miles per hour he reaches his igloo at 7.00pm. Next day taking the same route back he leaves his igloo with a sledge drawn by his husky, also at 3 miles per hour. Leaving at 4.00pm and reaching the bear at 7.00pm does Hubert pass the same point at the same time on the journey to and from the igloo?

Question 142 AQUEDUCT

The Emperor of Byzantium wanted to build an aqueduct to provide fresh water for the provincial city of Antioch. The source lay 40 miles away and at first the terrain ran downhill. However, the final stretch was uphill. Is it possible for water to flow uphill?

Question 143 MUSICAL MUDDLES

Professor Quaver of the Music Academy got his lecture notes back to front and allowed one unrelated topic to slip in. Can you find the odd one out – TRAZOM, HCAB, OSSACIP, RENGAW, RELHAM?

Question 144 ARTISTIC ANAGRAMS

Connect the names in group A with the items in group B.

group A: Shakespeare, Marlowe, Mozart, Milton
group B: mailbeermat, nilebymce, rapideas stol, lefötuberaz.

Question 145 TRAINS

Trains run from A to B one a minute, 24 hours a day. Trains run from B to A at the same rate with the journey taking one hour. Travelling from A to B how many trains do you pass?

Question 146 BEAKERS

Seven beakers stand in a row. Number 1 is empty, 2, 3 and 4 are full, while 5, 6 and 7 are empty. What is the quickest way to rearrange the beakers in order to leave them alternately empty and full?

BRAIN FLASH: World Chess Champion Alexander Alekhine could challenge 28 master-strength players at one and the same time and still win the majority of games, without seeing the board or pieces.

Question 147 PRIESTS

In the 100 step Ziggurat of Ur, priests gathered for the sacrifice to the memory of the hero Gilgamesh. The High Priest stood along on the top step, then two acolytes on the second, with the lower priests three on the third, four on the fourth and so on down to the 100th step. However, one priest heading for the bottom step was delayed by an earlier sacrifice at the Temple of Enkidu and did not make it. How many priests were at the ceremony?

Question 148 GOBLINS

On the island of Erewhon the Goblin population, thought to be near extinction, has expanded enormously. We know now two facts about them:

a) There are 400 goblins
b) No goblin has more than 150 wrinkles on his face.

From this can we deduce that there must be two goblins with the same number of wrinkles?

Question 149 USED CARS

Beauregarde's Used Cars were offering second hand vehicles for £1,000 plus 50% of each car's price. How much did the cars cost?

Question 150 ORIENT EXPRESS

The Orient Express leaves P at the same time as the Romanian Flyer departs from B. The Orient Express travels at 150 kilometres per hour, while the Romanian Flyer speeds along at 175 kilometres per hour. Which train is further from P when they pass?

Question 151 — ONE WORD ANSWER

What do the following words have in common?

DVA, DEUX, ZWEI, DUE, DOS

Question 152 — GREEDY

At Dotheboys Hall Comprehensive School each child is given a bag of sweets containing two gobstoppers, two sherbets, two jelly babies and two caramels. During the morning break seven tenths eat a gobstopper, 85% a sherbet, four fifths a caramel and three quarters a jelly baby. What is the minimum percentage of children who must have eaten all four?

Question 153 — PHILOSOPHY

At his philosophy lectures Professor Synapse gave papers on TANK, TOPAL, RISOLETTA, SNUBER and TTTNNEEIIWSG. Which topic was out of place?

Question 154 — VAMPIRE EXPRESS

The Transylvanian Flyer is travelling on a 300km stretch of track across central Europe. After 200 kms the train breaks down and the passengers have to transfer to the Vlad Puffer, a much slower local locomotive. The final 100km takes twice as long as the first 200km. How many times faster was the Transylvanian Flyer than the Vlad Puffer?

BRAIN FLASH: 'The human brain is an enchanted loom where millions of flashing shuttles weave a dissolving pattern, always a meaningful pattern, though never an abiding one. It is as if the Milky Way entered upon some cosmic dance.' Sir Charles Sherrington.

Question 155 BRIGHT IDEAS

Rearrange the following so that they match:

EINSTEIN – MICROSOFT
DODGSON – GRAVITY
GOETHE – RELATIVITY
NEWTON – LOOKING GLASS
GATES – FAUST.

Question 156 FARMER'S DILEMMA

Farmer Giles has to cross a narrow bridge with three sensitive items, but he can only carry one at a time. They are: hungry rabbit, ravenous cat and tasty carrots. Given that the cat will eat the rabbit if given the chance, while the rabbit will devour the carrots if they are left unattended, how does he solve his problem?

Question 157 CONFUSED CAPITALS

Rearrange the following so that they match:
AUSTRALIA – VIENNA
DENMARK – HELSINKI
AUSTRIA – COPENHAGEN
S. KOREA – CANBERRA
FINLAND – SEOUL

Question 158 CIRCLES

A triangle is composed of ten circles on four levels. Level 1 at the top has one circle, A. Level 2 has two, B and C. Level three has three, D, E and F, while level four has four, G, H, I and J. What is the minimum number of circles that need to be rearranged so that the apex of the triangle appears at the bottom?

Question 159 WISE WORDS

Who famously said:

Veni, Vidi, Vici	a) Julius Caesar,	b) Rene Descartes
Arma virumque cano	a) Virgil	b) Nero
Qualis artifex pereo	a) Virgil	b) Nero
Cogito ergo sum	a) Caligula	b) Descartes.

Question 160 ROMAN MATHS

Divide LXXX by XX, multiply by C and add DC. What is the final figure?

Question 161 EQUILATERAL

An equilateral triangle has the number 2 at the top, 6 bottom left and 4 bottom right. How do you place the numbers 8, 10, 12, 14, 16 and 18 along the sides so that each side adds up to 34?

Question 162 CUSTER'S LAST STAND

The night before the Battle of the Little Big Horn Colonel Custer dreamed that he was surrounded in a pure circle by 12 braves and one Indian chief. He had just 13 rounds of ammunition left and could only scare off the attackers by firing around the circle in one direction, either clockwise of anticlockwise, firing at every 13th assailant. As each Indian was scared off, the size of the circle was reduced by one. The chief had to be saved for the final shot. Where did Custer start so that each bullet was used to maximum effect?

Question 163 PRONOUNCE THIS

It is obvious how the word 'ghoti' should be pronounced – or is it? Can you justify the pronunciation 'fish'?

Question 164 SILENCE

Following on from the previous question, that word 'ghoti' could also be completely silent. Can you justify this?

Question 165 EXCHANGE RATE

If 12 zloty equal 16 ley, how many zloty for 72 ley?

Question 166 ORDER

Put the following in correct order, starting with the closest to a very large object:

HATER, RAMS, PRETJUI, SNUVE, NATURS, CRUMYER.

Question 167 SUBTRACTION

If you subtract the number of red cards in a normal pack of cards from the number of dark squares on a chessboard, what number is left?

BRAIN FLASH: 'When Richard Feynman was a youngster, his mother asked the future Nobel Prize winner the same question every evening at the dinner table. – "What did you ask at school today?"' – Thinking for a Change, Michael Gelb.

Question 168 RUSSIANS

General Jackson wants to deploy his divisions to neutralise the presence of the Russians. He orders the 4th para to go to the north of the 3rd para and northwest of the Russians. The Russians are southeast of the 4th para and northeast of the hussars. The tank regiment is northeast of the 3rd para and west of 2nd para. Which troop deployment is north of the Russians?

Question 169 UNGULATES

LUBL is to WOC as TAGS is to WEE, ODE, SWO or CKBU? (Hint: think ungulates!)

Question 170 ALPHANUMERICAL

If Z + A = 27 and X multiplied by Y = 6 what is I plus T minus M?

Question 171 BATH TIME

Water from a cold tap will take 30 minutes to fill a 600 litre bath. From a hot tap it will take 40 minutes. The full bath takes 50 minutes to empty. If the bath is empty and the plug is out and both the hot and cold taps are turned on, how long will it take to fill the bath?

Question 172 BULL

Cock is to bull as stuff is to ???????

Question 173 CHARLES

If Elizabeth = 3 and George = 21, what do Richard and Charles equal?

Question 174 POLITICIANS

Professor Politicus has mixed up leaders and residences. Can you help him out?

Casa Rosada, The Kremlin, The White House, 10 Downing Street.
Boris Yeltsin, Bill Clinton, Tony Blair, General Galtieri.

Question 175 I CANNAE DO IT CAPTAIN

Three starships enter space dock. They each need repairs to the hyperdrive and photon torpedo replenishment. There are two teams of star mechanics available, A and B, who operate equally swiftly. It takes 15 hours to repair hyperdrive and five hours each to arm each starship with photon torpedoes. How quickly can the whole job be done?

Question 176 FAIR BET

Fred and Joe both have £1,000. Fred bets Joe £100 that if Joe gives Fred £200 Fred will give him £300 back.If the transaction proceeds, who will benefit?

Question 177 HUNTING

A hunter chases a bear for three miles due North and then due South for a further two miles. What is the maximum distance he can be from where he began the hunt?

Question 178 IMPERIAL WATERS

The Tsar of Russia wanted to fill his ornamental miniature lake with 400 gallons of water. However, the Imperial water trucks only took 300 or 500 gallons. How could the Tsar engineers measure exactly 400 gallons?

Question 179 TROOP LOSSES

As Napoleon retreated from Moscow he was pursued by General Janvier through deep snow and blinding blizzards. At the first skirmish General Janvier lost 20% of his troops. At the second skirmish he lost 20% of those left. If he lost 7,200 men in total how many did he start with?

Question 180 AERONAUTICS

An aeroplane has a speed of 600 mph in still air. It makes a return journey between two points, one leg against a wind of 100 mph and the other with a tailwind, also of 100 mph. What is the average speed over the two journeys?

Question 181 HORSE RACE

A rich sheikh has four sons and three daughters, all equestrians. Upon his death they are to have a horse race. The last horse across the finishing line will inherit his fortune. How do they run the race?

Question 182 HUNGRY RHINOS

Six rhinos can devour six bales of hay in six minutes. The zookeeper gathers 100 bales of hay in his store room and leaves them unguarded for one hour and forty minutes. When he returns all the hay has been consumed. How many rhinos were guilty?

Question 183 ANCIENT AGES

The Cornelius family in Ancient Rome was famous for its longevity. Gaius Cornelius was born in 50BC. Which birthday would he have celebrated in 50AD?

Question 184 ANIMAL LOVERS

Re-arrange the following famous animal lovers in appropriate pairs:

Hannibal – Cats
T.S.Eliot – Elephants
Hemingway – Apes
Darwin – Big Game.

Question 185 COIN TOSS

Three boys play at tossing a coin. The winner is the first to throw a head. Andrew goes first, Bob second and Colin third. What are their chances?

Question 186 MATCHSTICK MANIA

V + I = II

How can the above equation be rectified by moving just one matchstick. (There are four possible answers.)

Question 187 OPPOSITES

Left is to right as top is to bottom, so black is to white as cameo is to ....?

Question 188 — APPOSITES

What specifically do these words have in common?

Pride, Unkindness, Murder.

Question 189 — WORD LINKS

Link the following words together:

Cheshire, Whittington, Archer, Stilton
Mayor, Cheese, Cat, Sherwood.

Question 190 — SIX VOWELS

Can you think of a word that contains six identical vowels?

Question 191 — ORDERED VOWELS

There are also three words which contain all five vowels in the correct order. What are they?

Question 192 — REVERSED VOWELS

Following on from this, there are also three words which feature the five vowels in reverse order. Can you think of them?

Question 193 HEAVY BALL

Given nine balls, identical except that one is slightly heavier than the rest, how can the odd one out be determined, using only two operations on a simple balancing scale?

Question 194 CLOCK HANDS

At precisely 6.00 a.m. the angle between the minute and hour hand of a clock is 180 degrees. To the nearest second, what time will it be when the angle between the two hands is again 180 degrees?

Question 195 THREE PIECE SUIT

If trousers and waistcoat cost £30, jacket and trousers cost £40 and waistcoat and jacket cost £32, how much is a three piece suit?

Question 196 AND

Can readers think of a type of sentence which has the word 'and' in it, five times consecutively?

Question 197 QUIZ SHOW

You are in a quiz show with a chance to win a million pounds by selecting the correct box from three. The host – and this is *very* important – knows which box contains the million. You make your choice and then the host opens one of the other boxes to reveal it as empty. He then offers you the chance to change your mind and select the remaining box. Should you do this?

Question 198 DATES

Professor Muddle has mixed up his historical dates. Can you help?

1066, 753BC, 1815, 1649
Battle of Waterloo, King Charles I executed, Battle of Hastings, Foundation of Rome.

Question 199 MATCHSTICK SQUARES

Can you arrange three matchsticks of equal length to form a square?

Question 200 THE PRISONER

Don Fernando, the cruelly capricious prison governor loves to torment his charges with tantalising tricks. He places prisoners A, B and C in cell 1 and prisoners D and E in cell 2. All prisoners know he has distributed a total of three white hats and two black hats to the prisoners and the distribution is as follows: A white; B white; C black; D black; E white. The prisoners can see their fellows' hats, but not their own. The first prisoner to identify the colour of their own hat gets double rations the following week. Which prisoners are in a position to identify their own hat?

two brains

QUESTIONS 201-300

Question 201 COUNT THE DAYS

Starting on January 1 and ending on December 31, what is the minimum number of days in ten years?

Question 202 REPETITION

Can you think of a sentence with the same word eleven times consecutively?

Question 203 SAND

If a bag of sand weighs 50 pounds divided by half its weight, how much does the bag weigh?

Question 204 IN TANDEM

Two people cycle round a track. One completes 16 circuits per hour and the other completes 10 circuits per hour. If they both start from the same point, how long will it be until they are together again?

Question 205 CRYPTIC CLUE

The letters ENTURY represent which well known saying?

BRAIN FLASH: The human memory can be quite astounding. Hiroyuki Goto (born 1973) of Tokyo, Japan, has memorised a staggering 42,195 digits of the number Pi, reciting them at the MHK Broadcasting Centre on 18 February 1995.

Question 206 LONGEST MONTH

longest?is the shortest month, but which is the

Question 207 SEQUENCE #11

What comes next in this sequence?

61, 52, 63, 94, 46, ??

Question 208 SNAIL'S PACE

Change SNAIL to SHELL in six steps, one letter at a time, creating a proper word at each stage.

Question 209 MURDERER

Who is reputed to have been responsible for killing a quarter of the world's population?

Question 210 TENNIS TOURNAMENT

82 players take part in a knockout tennis tournament. 18 first round matches reduce the field to 64 who then continue in normal knockout fashion. How many matches are played in total?

Question 211 'N'S

If the first thirty numbers are listed in words (i.e. one, two, three etc), how many 'n's are there?

Question 212 CRICKET

Which prominent cricketer has the surname of a sea spelt backwards?

Question 213 A-F

The first six letters of the alphabet appear in only four words. One of these is BIFURCATED. Can you think of the other three?

Question 214 A-G

Following on, there is a slightly contrived hyphenated word which contains the first seven letters. Can you think of it?

Question 215 ALPHABETICAL

And can you find six letter words in which the letters appear in alphabetical order?

Question 216 VENUES

Starting in 1948, which city follows London, Helsinki, Melbourne, Rome?

Question 217 PERFECT SQUARES

It is a perfect square, it is a three digit number. If you rotate it through 180 degrees it is also a perfect square. If you swap the last two digits it is also a perfect square. What is it?

Question 218	SEQUENCE #12

What is the next number in this sequence?

1485, 1509, 1547, 1553, ????

Question 219	THREE DIGITS

It is a three digit number. It is palindromic, it is a perfect square, the sum of the digits is prime. What is it?

Question 220	SEQUENCE #13

What is the missing number in the sequence?

??, 49, 36, 18, 8

Question 221	ODD ONE

Which of the following is the odd one?

bear – borne
do – done
fly – flown
mow – mown
shear – shorn

Question 222	DIFFERENCE

What is the difference between a cob and a pen?

Question 223 EVEN DATES

Wednesday 2 February 2000 can be expressed exclusively with even numbers (considering zero to be even), e.g. 2/2/2000. When was the previous time that happened?

Question 224 CLEVER BIRD

Which bird is reputed to have the highest IQ?

Question 225 COLLECTIVE NOUNS

Flock, fleet and flight – to what do these terms refer as collective nouns?

Question 226 BIRTHDAYS

Peter and his teenage grand-daughter Gemma share the same birthday. This year it was noted that the square of Peter's age was equal to the cube of Gemma's age. How old is Peter?

Question 227 LOCATION

Positions can be defined by 3 figure bearings measured clockwise from North, e.g. East = 090. My position is 7 degrees clockwise from North. Who am I?

Question 228 FOUR DIGITS

It is a four digit number. It is a perfect square. It reads the same upside down. Its square root is a prime number. What is it?

Question 229 STRANGE NUMBER

What is very strange about the number 6174 which makes it unique amongst four digit numbers? (It is to do with repeated subtractions.)

Question 230 NEPTUNE

Neptune is to Poseidon as Ceres is to ....?

Question 231 SPECIAL LETTERS

What does it take to write the following poem, and which two letters are special?

go in june dear
go pick some very small quantity of precious azure stone
and weave all together with a braid
bind fix or die

Question 232 REVERSED SQUARE

Which number when reversed and squared will give its own squared value in reverse?

Question 233 PLOUGH-BOY

'The dough-faced plough-boy coughed and hiccoughed his rough way through the borough'. What is unusual about this sentence?

Question 234 EN FRANCAIS

The following is a difficult question. What is the longest single word palindrome in French? (Hint: think of commandos.)

Question 235 DOCTORS ORDERS

'Doc – note, I dissent, a fast never prevents a fatness – I diet on cod'. What is unusual about this sentence?

Question 236 NO REPETITION

What is the longest word you can come up with which does not repeat any letters? The answer gives a word which is 16 letters long.

Question 237 AD INFINITUM

What is the significance of the following infinitely recurring sequence?

1, 4, 9, 6, 5, 6, 9, 4, 1, 0, 1, 4, 9, 6, 5, 6, 9, 4, 1, 0 ....

Question 238 NEXT PLEASE

What follows next in this sequence?

QAZ, WSX, EDC, RFV, TGB, ???

BRAIN FLASH: 'If you want to get a good idea, get a lot of ideas!' – Dr Linus Pauling, two-time Nobel prize winner.

Question 239 REWRITE

How could the following statement be rewritten so as to make sense?

X, Y, D, TTT and 7 all eventually end in C.

Question 240 DAYS OLD

On his birthday in 1992 Dr. Primes was intrigued to note that his age in years multiplied by the day in the year (considered numerically with 1 January equalling one) came to 11,111. What was his age and date of birth?

Question 241 LONG JOURNEY

Imagine that you start a journey from a fixed point and proceed as follows: you travel 1,000 miles north, 1,000 miles east, 1,000 miles south and 1,000 miles west. What are the answers to the following two questions?

At what point must you begin your journey in order to arrive back at exactly the same point at which you departed?

Question 242 NO WAY

And what starting points make it impossible to complete such a journey?

Question 243 UNUSUAL WORDS

What do the words 'Silver', 'Purple', 'Orange' and 'Month' have in common?

Question 244 REFRESHMENT

What refreshment can be made from WINTER COAT?

Question 245 ETA

If I arrive at Trafalgar Square at five past six in the evening, what time do I get to Waterloo?

Question 246 SERIES #3

Give the next two terms in the following series:

a) UDTQC
b) LMMJV

Question 247 LAZY DOG

The well known sentence which contains all the letters of the alphabet is 'The quick brown fox jumped over the lazy dog'. This is 36 letters long. There is an example, given in the solution, which is 32 letters long. Can you do as well, or better? The sentence must be meaningful.

Question 248 MILLENIAL AGE

Catherine's birthday has just passed and she has given birth very recently. The year's calendar (2000) is exactly the same as the one when she was born. How old is Catherine?

Question 249 COMMON WORDS

What do the following have in common?

CALMNESS, CANOPY, DEFT, FIRST, SIGHING, STUPID.

Question 250 HEAVIER

Which is heavier, an ounce of gold or an ounce of sugar?

Question 251 REMARKABLE NUMBERS

The number 153 is remarkable because 1 (raised to the 3) + 5 (raised to the 3) + 3 (raised to the 3) = 153. Why is 54748 remarkable?

Question 252 ANALYSE THIS

Explain the following:
woo ten, true of her, if vex is, given sheet, teen inn, new velvet eel.

Question 253 SERIES #4

What comes next: F4E, S9, SE5EN ?

Question 254 CONSECUTIVE VOWELS

What is the only English word which contains five consecutive vowels?

Question 255 TEMPERATURE

100 degrees Celsius is equivalent to 212 degrees Fahrenheit and 0 degrees Celsius is equivalent to 32 degrees Fahrenheit. What is the only temperature which is expressed in the same number of degrees on both scales?

Question 256 REVOLUTIONS

What is your best estimate for the number of complete revolutions a 5p coin would make to roll the full width of a twenty pound note?

Question 257 PHONE HOME

Martians need 21,300 miles of cable to lay a telephone wire around their equator. How much more cable would they need to hang the wire on six inch telegraph poles?

Question 258 REMARKABLE EQUATION

What is remarkable about the following equation?

11 + 2 = 12 + 1

BRAIN FLASH: 'My experience, in both government and industry, has demonstrated to me that those who are mind sports enthusiasts bring a special dimension of intellectual acumen and competitive drive to their professional activities' – Sir Brian Tovey, former Director General of GCHQ, the government communications centre. Chess masters Harry Golombek, C. H. O' D. Alexander and Sir Stuart Milner-Barry, were all prominent at the Bletchley Park code-breaking centre in World War II.

Question 259 — SCIENCE

Why do many science students find it useful to learn this sentence: 'How I like a drink, alcoholic of course, after the heavy lectures involving quantum mechanics'?

Question 260 — GOING UNDERGROUND

Which is the only London Underground station that does not include a letter from the word 'Mackerel'?

Question 261 — TELEPHONE NUMBERS

At the time when telephone numbers consisted of both letters and numbers why should the then Duke of Malborough's number have been BROM4689?

Question 262 — SPIDERS

If five spiders can catch five flies in five minutes.

a) How long would it take 100 spiders to catch 100 flies?
b) How many flies would 100 spiders catch in 100 minutes?

Question 263 — OCCUPATIONS

What have the occupations of blacksmith, fishmonger, lumberjack and journalist in common with my friend Mr. Mackintosh?

Question 264 — ICELAND C

In the armed services during the second world war, Iceland was officially known as Iceland (c). Why was this a dashed good idea?

Question 265 — YOLK

Is it more correct to say 'yolk is white' or 'yolk are white'?

Question 266 — NOTHING IN COMMON

Why have the following words got nothing in common?

naughtiness, senility, cloverleaf, shelducks.

Question 267 — PRIME NUMBERS

It is possible to make numerous nine digit numbers which comprise each of the nine digits used once each (e.g. 392874651). How many of these numbers are prime?

Question 268 — DECIPHER

Can you make sense of this?

YYURYYUBICURYYIVME

Question 269 — COMMONALITY

What have the following words in common?
xenophobic, weird, vile, thieving, selfish.

BRAIN FLASH: The most celebrated Mind Sports tragedy occurred in Kansas 1931 when John Bennett played a friendly hand of bridge with his wife against their neighbours, the Hoffmans. Mr Bennett played so badly that his wife left the room, returned with a pistol and shot him dead. Mrs Bennett was tried for murder but acquitted!

Question 270 PATHWAY

Form a series of words from GATE to DOOR via PATH in seven moves, changing one letter per move and forming proper words at each step.

Question 271 REDUCED WORDS

Can you think of two examples of nine letter words which have the following property? You can remove one letter at a time (i.e. leaving eight letters, then seven, then six etc.) in such a way that all the remaining combinations of letters make valid words.

Question 272 CROPPED WORDS

Following on, there are two nine letter examples which break all the way down to a one letter word, but only knock off letters at the beginning or end of the words. Can you find them?

Question 273 AGE SQUARED

When was the last year in which someone could have been born in order to live in a year which was the square of their age?

Question 274 CRYPTIC

Can you make sense of this?

If the B mt put: If the B. putting:

Question 275 DISTRIBUTION

Catherine has nine sweets and four bags. How can she distribute the sweets so that she has an odd number of sweets in each bag?

Question 276 MILLENIAL BIRTHDAY

Adding your age after your year 2000 birthday to the year you were born will give the total 100. When will this next happen?

Question 277 MONTHS

Why are September, October, November and December all two out?

Question 278 COLLECTIONS

Match the words in the following two collections:

Pea, Key, Sea, Swans, Whales, Locusts, Handel
Salt, Concerto, Green, Pod, Swarm, Fleet, Door.

Question 279 PUNGENT

Pungent is to taste as .... is to sound?

Is it muted, cacophonous, muffled or deafening?

BRAIN FLASH: 'Many people say they are thinking, when they are only rearranging their prejudices.' – William James, philosopher.

Question 280 ANGELS

In the Paradiso Canto XXVIII vv 92-93 Dante wrote: 'There were so many angels that their quantity would surpass the number you would achieve by the geometrical process of doubling the chess squares.' (i.e. 1st square = 1, 2nd square = 2, 3rd square = 4 etc.). What was the number of angels?

Question 281 BRICKS

If a brick weighs three pounds plus the weight of half-a-brick, what does a brick-and-a-half weigh?

Question 282 USAGE

Four uses four; five uses five; six uses six. Seven merely uses three, whereas only eight uses all seven. With this information, say how many do one and two use?

Question 283 DOUBLE LETTERS

What word contains three consecutive sets of double letters?

Question 284 KEY

What is the key to the following sequence?

E T A O I N S H R D L U

Question 285 SYLLABLES

Can you think of a one syllable word that converts to a three syllable word by the insertion of only one extra letter?

Question 286 — SEQUENCE #14

What is the next number in this sequence?

1, 2, 3, 7, 22

Question 287 — FOUR LETTER WORDS

Can you find six four letter words which use the same four letters?

Question 288 — FIFTIES

After 1957 comes 1958 and then 1959. If 1960 is not next, what is?

Question 289 — COMMON LINK

What is the common link between these words?

house, pure, kitchen, swear, dribble, desk

Question 290 — THE FOUR SEASONS

In Great Britain the four seasons are of exactly the same length, but in France spring is much longer than summer, why?

Question 291 — EXPANDED WORDS

Can you change the word 'rot' to 'resurrection' by adding one letter at each stage? You are allowed to make anagrams of the previous words, e.g. you can add an 'n' and make 'torn'.

Question 292 SEQUENCE #15

Which is the next letter in the following sequence?

M V E M J S U N

Question 293 BATTLES

Which two important battles were separated by exactly 300 years?

Question 294 DISCREPANCIES

Actually the answer to the previous question is not strictly correct. Why not?

Question 295 WILDLIFE

What do the following have in common: the ring-tailed cat, the crayfish, the firefly, the glass snake, the horned toad and the civet cat?

Question 296 RACETRACK

Can you name an obscure town, which used to be known for National Hunt racing, which contains half the letters of the alphabet?

BRAIN FLASH: 'It is possible that the capacity of the dolphin brain offers it a potential for memorising maps of ocean geography. The dolphin may see sound. It is an extraordinary fact that some people who are unusually gifted with memory may actually talk of hearing colour and seeing sound.' Professor Michael Crawford.

Question 297 FOREIGN NUMBERS

What do the following numbers have in common in their various languages?
four (English), vier (German), tre (Italian) and cinco (Spanish).

Question 298 PECULIAR SENTENCE

What is peculiar about the following sentence?

'Roman court chose a coin or pain'.

Question 299 SIX LETTER WORDS

Can you find seven six letter words which all use the same letters?

Question 300 PRESIDENTIAL ELECTION

Can you change BUSH to GORE in five steps, changing one letter at a time and making valid words on the way?

two brains

QUESTIONS 301-400

Question 301 MEDIA

In what medium could two Es be said to make an I, two Is be said to make an H, and two Ts be said to make an M?

Question 302 SERIES #5

Which is the next number in the series?

2, 4, 6, 30, 32, 34, 36, 40, 42, 44, 46, 50, 52, 54, 56, 60, 62, 64, 66, ?

Question 303 DIY

In a DIY store I can buy one for £1, ten for £2 and one hundred for £3. What are they?

Question 304 FIVE VOWELS

Can you think of a nine letter word which has the same vowel five times plus four consonants?

Question 305 PECULIAR PIETY

What is peculiar about the following pious hope?
'May the sin of usury not win rewards'

BRAIN FLASH: In 1879 in Virginia, USA Thomas Fuller (when he was about 79 years old) calculated mentally the number of seconds elapsed in any given time period. For example, for 70 years, 17 days and 12 hours the correct answer was given in one and a half minutes: 2,210,500,800 (assuming a 365¼ day year).

Question 306 ANALOGUE

On an ordinary analogue watch or clock face, how many times will the minute hand pass completely over the hour hand in twelve hours, starting at 12 noon?

Question 307 FOUR VOWELS

Can you think of a 13 letter word which features the same vowel four times and has only three other consonants?

Question 308 ODD COMBINATION

Match the following five words:

stone, part, brim, nut, cross

with these:

ridge, bill, chat, hatch, stone

and then decide which combination is the odd one out.

Question 309 PLURALS

Most nouns in the English language are pluralised by the addition of an 's'. Can you find a common word, that with the addition of an 's' is not only turned from a plural into a singular, but also changes gender?

Question 310 COMMON LETTERS

What do the following have in common?

bg, dn, ht, pp, pt, tn

Question 311 SIX CONSONANTS

Form words from each of the following by inserting six consonants and a hyphen:

SI******EEN, CA******ASE, WA******AP.

Question 312 APPEARANCES

Can you think of two English words that look like opposites but actually have the same meaning?

Question 313 FROM A TO B

It takes three days to go from A to B, but four days to go from B to A. Name A and B.

Question 314 ABBREVIATION

What well known abbreviation, when spoken, uses twice as many syllables as the three words it stands for?

Question 315 TIMEPIECE

Which timepiece has the greatest number of moving parts?

Question 316 RESOLUTIONS

What New Year resolution is impossible to keep and yet also impossible to break?

Question 317 THE KNOWLEDGE

Can you think of a well known London thoroughfare of 13 letters which has only three vowels?

Question 318 ONE AND A HALF

Simon is one and a half times as old as Niall, who is one and a half times as old as David. Their ages total 152 years. How old is Niall?

Question 319 TRANSLATE

Can you make sense of this:

'Oyo is an imyant y in Yugal which exys y'.

Question 320 COMMON THEME

What do the following have in common?

Hand, point, foot, water.

Question 321 COMPLETION

The sequence plead, label, album, lusty, ????? is completed by which of the following words?

frown, lunch, until, launch.

Question 322 SPECIAL DAY

Dates can be represented in several ways using three numbers, e.g. 24 March 2001 can be 2431, 240301, 1324 or 010324. Using all four methods what makes 4th April 2001 a special day?

Question 323 UNUSUAL LETTERS

What's so very unusual about the letters in the words LIMNOPHILOUS (living in ponds or marshes) and UNDERSTUDY?

Question 324 ADDITION

What do the following words have in common?

herd, sent, sty, rein, our, new, by, rest

Question 325 COLD WEATHER

How can tin, oxygen and tungsten make the weather colder?

Question 326 BATHROOM

What kind of bathroom might the following numbers suggest to a Frenchman: 11, 8?

BRAIN FLASH: 'If anything is good for the mind, it is memory training. Memory training develops all cortical skills and trains the whole of the brain using both hemispheres. The techniques of using association, imagination and location employ all elements of the brain.' Dominic O'Brien, World Memory Champion.

Question 327	ASSOCIATIONS

Put the following together:

Columbus, Marlowe, Goethe, Gutenberg, da Vinci

Mona Lisa, Bible, America, Faust, Tamberlaine.

Question 328	DEAD CROWS

100 crows are perched at evenly spaced intervals on a telegraph wire. Ted, Joe and Dan fire simultaneously at the crows. Ted kills all the crows on the first one fifth of the wire, Joe kills 10% of the remainder, whilst Dan kills all birds on 20% of the length of the wire. How many birds remain on the wire?

Question 329	PALINDROMES

The word 'reviver' is a palindrome, i.e. reads the same forwards as backwards. Can you think of a seven letter palindrome which contains four vowels?

Question 330	REVERSIBLE LETTERS

The letters A, H, I, M and O are reversible in that they are unaltered if viewed from behind. In what context are D, N, R and U the only reversible letters?

Question 331	DUPUYTREN'S CONTRACTURE

Both Margaret Thatcher and Ronald Reagan suffer from the medical condition Dupuytren's Contracture. (This causes clawing of the fingers and affects the ability to type.) What is unusual about Dupuytren's Contracture?

Question 332 FLOATING

I am reclining on a lilo, alone in a swimming pool. I am holding a brick on my lap which I then release into the water where it obviously sinks to the bottom. Does the water level in the pool rise slightly, stay the same or go down slightly?

Question 333 APPROACH AND IDENTIFY

Identify the following and connect them:

a) A unit of pressure
b) A Manchester United hero in Barcelona
c) A palindromic woman
d) A 'satisfactory' GCSE 'pass'
e) A Shakespearean king

Question 334 MILKING

If you were milking a cow, how far away would you be from the nearest religious book?

Question 335 VALUES

If R=80, C=100 and K=373, what is the value of F?

Question 336 CATTLE

A farmer died leaving three sons. He bequethed the first son half of his cattle, the second one third and to the third son one ninth. He had 17 cows in total. How did they solve the problem of dividing up the cattle?

Question 337 POPULATION

Two fathers and two sons leave a town. The population only goes down by three. Why?

Question 338 SECURITY

Alan needs to some Bill some important documents which must be secured in a chest with a padlock. However, the courier company is unreliable and will steal anything that is not in a locked chest (e.g. a key sent separately will be stolen). Alan has various padlocks and keys, as does Bill. How can they coordinate to transfer the documents safely?

Question 339 CIRCUMNAVIGATION

A ship leaves a dock, and travels right around the world arriving back at its original starting place exactly. In exactly the same place it started from. Which part of the ship travelled the furthest?

Question 340 OAK TREE

A young oak tree had ten branches. In May each branch grew 60 leaves. Each of the following months it grew 10 more leaves on each branch. How many leaves would it have seven months later?

BRAIN FLASH: The IQ test was originated by Alfred Binet (1857-1911) as an objective measure of comprehension, reasoning and judgment. Binet was motivated by a powerful enthusiasm for the emerging discipline of psychology and a desire to overcome the cultural and class prejudices of late 19th century France in the assessment of children's academic potential.

Question 341 BANKRUPTCY

A man pushes his car along until he stops in front of a hotel. He suddenly realises that he is bankrupt. How can this be?

Question 342 TWICE

Make the longest word you can from the letters N,A,S,I,T,E. You can't use any letter twice.

Question 343 DRINKS MACHINE

A drinks machine has three options: tea, coffee and random. A friend tells you that the machine is faulty and that the buttons are never correct. Each drink is 50p. How much money would you need to spend to know which buttons deliver which drinks?

Question 344 EGG TIMER

It's breakfast time and you need to boil an egg. It must be boiled for nine minutes and you have only a 4 minute and a 7 minute egg timer. How can you do the egg?

Question 345 MISSING GLOVE

A man is wearing a suit and one glove. He is dead, why?

Question 346 LOAVES

A man goes into a bakers shop and puts 50p on the counter. 'Brown or white?' asks the shop assistant. Later that day another man comes in and again puts 50p on the counter. This time the shop assistant knows for sure that he wants a brown loaf. How?

Question 347 — DEPTHS OF WATER

Equal weights are dropped simultaneously from the same height into buckets on the ground. The first has 4 inches of water at 40 degrees Fahrenheit and the second has 3 inches of water at 30 degrees Fahrenheit. Which reaches the bottom of the bucket first?

Question 348 — NEWTONIAN PHYSICS

In a balloon, stationary off the coast of Ireland, I dropped two wine bottles off the side. If one was full, and the other empty, which hit the ground first?

Question 349 — CAR PARK

Lenny has just parked in a car park and needs to remember the location. The spaces to the left read 16, 06, 68, 88 and the one on the right is 98. What number did he park his car?

Question 350 — JASON

Why is Jason not a man for all seasons?

Question 351 — GENDER BENDER

Which seven letter word starts masculine, changes to feminine, then back to masculine and ends up feminine?

BRAIN FLASH: In 1923 psychometrician C. M. Cox estimated the greatest historical IQs in his *Genetic Studies of Genius*. His conclusions were as follows: 1 Goethe 210; 2 Leibnitz 205; 3-4 Newton and Pitt the Younger both 190; 5 Galileo 185. Notable omissions from his list were da Vinci, Shakespeare and Einstein, who have variously been estimated as respectively 220, 210 and 205.

Question 352 SHOPPING

A woman catches the train to go shopping each week. She can go to Eastlea or Westlea and doesn't mind which. Trains for both destinations arrive every ten minutes and she always catches the first available train. Why does she end up in Westlea nine weeks out of ten?

Question 353 QWERTY

Which 10 letter word can be composed using only the first line of letters on a keyboard (QWERTYUIOP) ?

Question 354 LIMITATIONS

In chess, there is one specific type of move which the queen is unable to make, but all the other pieces can. What is it?

Question 355 NEAT NUMBERS

If ANTE minus ETNA equals NEAT (all four-digit numbers), what digits are represented by A, N, T and E?

Question 356 SHOEBOX

A shoe box measures 10 inches x 4 x 4. A fly is sitting centrally on the top of one end, while a spider is waiting opposite, on the bottom, at the other end. What distance must the spider cover to catch the fly?

Question 357 COINS

John took some coins from his money box and arranged them in the following way:
£2, 50p, 2p, £1, 20p, 1p, 5p.
Why?

Question 358 AMOUNTS

Why is the sum £8.88 special?

Question 359 PENSIONER

John is an old age pensioner. Reversing the digits of his age this year and doubling the answer gives his age next year. How old is John?

Question 360 TWO BRAINS

In the following, each capital letter has a consistent value. Can you work them out?

[KEENE + BRAIN] times 4 = WEEKLY

Question 361 PUNCH THE CLOCK

A clock strikes the hour every hour and also strikes just once every 15 minutes. If you can only hear the clock what is the longest time you can wait before being completely certain what the correct time is?

Question 362 SHAPES AND COLOURS

How are a red triangle, a purple square, an orange diamond and a green circle related?

Question 363 EQUATE THIS

How can the following be made true with the addition of one line?

5 + 5 + 5 = 550

Question 364 SQUARE AGES

This year my father's age, my son's age and my daughter's age are all square numbers. When my daughter was born, my age was also a square number and exactly the same as my father's age when I was born. How old am I now?

Question 365 SERIES #6

The following is part of a commonly encountered series of digits: 10111212. What immediately precedes it?

Question 366 HOCUS POCUS

What do the letters represent in the following addition?

HOCUS + POCUS = PRESTO.

Question 367 OIL GAUGE

A train is travelling at 100 miles per hour. There is a spot of oil on one wheel. What speed is this spot doing, in relation to the ground, when it reaches its highest point?

Question 368 SAME SOUNDS

Can you think of four English words which are pronounced the same but all spelt differently?

Question 369 DIFFERENT LETTERS

Can you think of a pair of English words that are pronounced the same but are spelled using entirely different letters?

Question 370 SAME MEANINGS

Can you think of a pair of English words which are spelt differently, but sound the same and have the same meaning?

Question 371 SEQUENCE #16

What is the next number in this sequence?

1, 8, 11, 69, 88, 96

Question 372 FIVE

Explain these five numbers:

1, 5, 9, 15, 21

Question 373 PAIRINGS

Explain the following pairings:

(1,3), (2,3), (3,5), (4,4), (5,4), (6,3), (7,5), (8,5), (9,4), (10,3).

Question 374 SURPRISING

What is remarkable about the following sentence?

'The picture shows an Englishwoman and two Asian women at work in a crowded North London shop.'

Question 375 SERIES #7

What is the next number in this series?

13, 44, 88, 176, 847, ???

Question 376 ANTONYMS

Can you think of any English words that can have two different, entirely opposite meanings?

Question 377 MULTIPLES

What is unusual about multiples of the number 142,857 ?

BRAIN FLASH: Many of us have experienced problems with mental calculation at school. However, William Klein in Rhode Island in 1982 when aged 70 multiplied two five-digit numbers mentally in 42 seconds. Try it for yourself before resorting to the calculator. The two numbers he was randomly given were: 57825 x 13489.

Question 378 AURAL ANAGRAMS

Can you think of three examples of pairs of five letter English words which are anagrams of each other and sound the same?

Question 379 ELEMENTARY MATHS

If 44 + 7 = RUN and 6 + 85 = CAT and 5 + 76 + 16 = BOSS, what does 35 + 33 + 16 equal?

Question 380 RECTANGLES

Imagine a four-by-four grid consisting of 16 squares. How many rectangles (including squares) of any size, does this contain?

Question 381 OBSERVATION

Where could you observe that:

1=2, 2=5, 3=5, 4=4, 5=5, 6=5, 7=3, 8=7 and 9=5 ?

Question 382 SEQUENCE #17

What are the next two in the following sequence: 95:E L5:E 85:E ?

Question 383 SIGNIFICANT DATES

What is the significance of the following dates in any non-leap year: April 10, July 19, October 27?

Question 384 COMMON PROPERTY

What do the following words have in common?

Deer, Dress, Look, Poll, Sew, Tresses, Was.

Question 385 EQUAL AND OPPOSITE

Can you think of two adjectives with opposite meanings, which, when used as verbs, mean the same thing?

Question 386 NO EIGHT

Why is the following number interesting?

12345679

(Hint: multiplication is the key.)

Question 387 REVERSED RHYME

Can you think of a word of three letters (all different) which, when reversed, provides another word, rhyming with the original?

BRAIN FLASH: Some people have an amazing ability to multiply giant numbers and calculate distant roots. On 18 June 1980, Shakuntala Devi multiplied together two 13 digits numbers in 28 seconds. They were 7,686,369,774,870 x 2,465,099,745,779. The answer by the way is 18,947,668,177,995,426,462,773,730. Mrs Devi also extracted the 23rd root of a 201 digit number in 50 seconds at the Southern Methodist University in Dallas, USA.

Question 388 NOT OUT

In a cricket match, each batsman is bowled out first ball. Who is the remaining not out batsman?

Question 389 SERIES #8

What are the next two letters in this series?

F, S, T, F, F, S, S, ?, ?

Question 390 DIGITAL CLOCK

Imagine a digital clock where you can only see the bottom three segments, as the upper four are obscured. For a 12-hour clock, what are the only times which can be read with no ambiguity?

Question 391 HOT OR COLD

Which word is this?

'Alone, I am cold. I become hot if you add the letter 'i' to me, but I turn cold again if you add 'y' instead'.

BRAIN FLASH: The US President and Congress declared the 1990's to be the 'Decade of the Brain'. 'Resolved by the Senate and House of Representatives of the United States of America in Congress Assembled, that the decade beginning January 1, 1990 hereby is designated the "Decade of the Brain", and the President of the United States is authorized and requested to issue a proclamation calling upon all public officials and the people of the United States to observe such decade with appropriate programs and activities.' Approved 25 July 1989.

Question 392 FIFTY PER CENT

What word uses over fifty per cent of the letters of the alphabet once and once only?

Question 393 THE MEDIUM IS...

In which medium could it be said that ONE = 6666633, SIX = 777744499, and FORTY = 3336667778999?

Question 394 WEDNESDAY TREAT

What remarkable event happened in the evening on the third Wednesday in February 2002?

Question 395 ONE HUNDRED

Using the numbers 1 to 9 in order and using only normal mathematical signs (add, subtract, multiply, divide and brackets) create an equation which sums to 100.

Question 396 MEASUREMENT

Name three units of measurement which sounds like three consecutive letters of the alphabet?

BRAIN FLASH: On 26 October 1991 at the Athenaeum, London, Frank Felberbaum of New York displayed perfect memorisation of US National League Baseball statistics from 1876 to 1990, covering year, winning team, manager, total winning games for the season and the winning percentage. This amounted to 2,000 differing pieces of information and data.

Question 397 — DIGITAL EQUATION

In the equation A x B = C, the ten digits 0 – 9 are used once each. Can you construct the equation?

Question 398 — PUNCTUATION

Can you punctuate the following sentence to make it make sense?

time flies you cannot their flight is too erratic

Question 399 — STATION CLOCK

Each digit display on the panel of a mechanical, digital, 24-hour, railway station clock, showing of mechanical:ss, has seven moving parts. At what time does the greatest number movements occur?

Question 400 — THIRTEEN TO FOUR

What word can represent half the letters of the alphabet, but is only four letters in length?

BRAIN FLASH: 'Alan Turing (1912-1954) dared to ask whether a machine could think. His contributions to understanding and answering this defy conventional classification. At the close of the twentieth century, the 1936 concept of the Turing Machine appears not only in mathematics and computer science, but in cognitive science and theoretical biology. His 1950 paper – Computing Machinery and Intelligence – describing the so-called Turing Test, is a cornerstone of the theory of artifical intelligence.' Turing by Andrew Hodges (published by Phoenix)

---

two brains

QUESTIONS 401-500

Question 401 — INFLATION

Why are 1997 50p coins worth more than 1996 50p coins?

Question 402 — NUMERICAL PROPERTY

The numbers 3, 7, 8, 40, 50 and 60 have a property in common which no other number has. What is that property?

Question 403 — COUNTING IN FRENCH

What comes next in this sequence?

un, deux, quatre, six, trois.

Question 404 — PUZZLING WORDS

I have two five letter words. I take the first letter of one and put it at the front of the other to make a four letter and a six letter word. The meaning of the four letter word has not changed, but the six letter word now means the opposite of its original. What are the original two words?

Question 405 — OXYGEN

As altitude increases what happens to the ratio of oxygen in the air?

a) It gets less and its becomes more difficult to breathe.
b) It increases.
c) It remains the same.

Question 406 — IN THE CHAIR

When you enter the Cabinet Room at 10 Downing Street how would you differentiate the chair of the Prime Minister from those of the Ministers?

Question 407 — THE LETTER X

Into which group of letters – and why – does the letter X go?

A B D F G H L Q R T

C K O P S U V W

Question 408 — HAVE WHAT?

Two have only one, four have two, nine have three and eleven have four. What does this refer to?

Question 409 — INSIDER DEALING

Two words are spelt differently but pronounced the same and you may well find some of one inside the other. What are they?

Question 410 — INSIDE AND UNDER

Two words are spelt and pronounced the same and you may well find some of one inside the other? What are they?

Question 411 THAT IS

Punctuate the following sentence to make sense:

that that is is that that is not is not is that it it is

Question 412 HOLD AND COLD

Alone I am hot. Take two letters away and I am cold. Take another away and I warm up a bit.

What am I?

Question 413 ODDS AND ENDS

Add a three letter sequence (identical for each example, although different in each case) to the beginning and end of the following to make complete words:

MEN
ICEM
***ERGRO**

Question 414 CAPITAL ANAGRAMS

Name an African country which is an anagram of a South American capital city.

Question 415 ALPHABETICAL ORDER

What is the longest English word which has its letters in alphabetical order?.

Question 416 FIVE SYLLABLES

Can you think of an eight letter word which consists of five syllables?

Question 417 IXAT

Suddenly I spotted an IXAT following me. Where was I?

Question 418 MISSING LETTER

What is the missing letter?

A, F, H, K, ?, Y, Z

Question 419 MISSING NUMBER

What is the missing number in this series?

5, 8, 3, ?, 2, 1

Question 420 BST

When British Summer time started this year I had to adjust all my timepieces. Although I did most of them around midnight, I had to leave one until after breakfast the next morning. Why?

BRAIN FLASH: 'Study the science of art and the art of science. Learn how to see and remember that everything is connected to everything else.' – Leonardo da Vinci.

Question 421 TOTAL DIGITS

If you write down all the possible numbers produced by the five digits 1, 3, 5, 7, 9 and then add them up, what is the total?

Question 422 MULTIPLICATION

How many terms do you get when you multiply out the following?

$(x - a)(x - b)(x - c).....(x - y)(x - z)$

Question 423 CONSONANT STRING

Which common English word contains the sequence 'tchst'? Which English placename contains the sequence 'ghtsbr'?

Question 424 DOUBLE H

Which English word contains the sequence 'hh'?

Question 425 POWERFUL CONSONANTS

What word, by the insertion of one consonant, changes its meaning from exercise power to abrogate power?

Question 426 HOW MANY

What word changes its meaning from 'approximately' to 'exactly' when you separate its first two letters?

Question 427 COUNTY

Which historic British county is spelt with three identical letters in sequence?

Question 428 OPPOSITE VOWELS

The meaning of two very common verbs can be converted to their exact opposites by substituting one vowel for another. What are they?

Question 429 THREE BY THREE

Can you complete this three by three square so that each column, row and diagonal totals 111?

```
x 1 x
x x x
x x x
```

Question 430 ANCIENT GREEK

An ancient Greek lived one-fourth of his life as a boy, one-fifth as a youth, one-third as a man and spent the last 13 years of his life as an elderly gent. How old was he when he died?

Question 431 ODOMETER

While driving his car, Bob notes that the reading on the odometer is a palindrome – 13,931 miles. Two hours later, he notices that the new reading is another palindrome. What is the most likely speed at which he has been travelling?

Question 432 HYPHENATION

What word changes its meaning from 'to be kept for use ahead of other people' to 'to be kept for use after other people' by inserting a hyphen?

Question 433 RISK OR REWARD

What eight letter word can mean a penalty or a reward?

Question 434 ODD AND EVEN

Which two odd numbers, when multiplied together, give a statement of an even number?

BRAIN FLASH: Practitioners of mind sports are fascinated by the relative difficulty of their different pastimes. The approximate number of possible positions available in the most popular mind sports is as follows. Shogi is the Japanese version of chess, in which captured pieces defect to the opposite side, while XiangQi is the type of chess played in China, where pieces include the elephant and a central river divides the board in two.

Go	10^{170}
Scrabble	10^{150}
Poker	10^{72}
Shogi	10^{70}
Chess	10^{50}
XiangQi	10^{50}
Bridge	10^{30}
Draughts	10^{20}
Backgammon	10^{19}

Question 435 EMOTIONS

Can you think of two words which both involve emotion? With the first, adding one letter at the end changes it from a noun to an adjective. With the second adding the same letter at the end changes it from an adjective to a noun.

Question 436 SCOTLAND

Wales has 15, Ireland has 7, England has 4. How many does Scotland have?

Question 437 FLOREAL AND NIVOSE

If Floreal is the second and Nivose is the seventh, what are the fourth and sixth?

Question 438 WATCHING

If you can see a knob, dopping, siege, sute and rush, what are you looking at?

Question 439 EDIBLE VOWELS

Can you think of a word which can be changed into its opposite by the addition of a vowel in the middle? (Hint: think of food.)

Question 440 HALF

If a man and a half build a house and a half in a year and a half, how long does it take one man to build one house?

Question 441 INSERTION

Place the remaining numbers 8 and 9 into one or other of the two lines below:

a) 1 2 4
b) 3 5 6 7

Question 442 TRACKING

What common word can lose either of its first two letters making three words with identical pronunciation?

Question 443 CAREERS

Which two words are synonyms when applied to a person's career, but are antonyms when applied to his character?

Question 444 MENTAL ARITHMETIC

How can you use the numbers 1, 3, 4 and 6 exactly once each, with the standard arithmetic operators (brackets, add, subtract, divide and multiply), to reach a total of 24?

Question 445 GIANTS

Where, in everyday life do you find the phrase 'Standing on the shoulders of giants'?

Question 446 INEDIBLE

Can you name a foodstuff that becomes uneatable if you remove a consonent?

Question 447 RELATIONSHIPS

In a room there is a man and a woman. The man's mother-in-law and the woman's mother-in-law are mother and daughter. What is the man's relationship to the woman?

Question 448 WINE

You have two glasses of wine, one white, one red. You stir a spoonful of the red into the white and then a spoonful of the white into the red. Which wine is now more polluted?

Question 449 UNRHYMING COUPLETS

Can you think of two words that do not rhyme and yet end in the same eight letters?

Question 450 TWO MORE

Name another two words which do not rhyme despite ending in the same six letters.

BRAIN FLASH: In April 1847, Johann Martin Dase was reported as having achieved the following calculations: multiplying two 20 digit numbers in six minutes, two 48 digit numbers in 40 minutes and, incredibly, two 100 digit numbers together in 8¾ hours (all these calculations performed mentally). Additionally, 2 x 8 digit numbers: 49,735,827 x 98,536,474 in one minute and seven seconds on paper. (Answer: 4,900,793,024,053,998). However, mentally he was even quicker with: 79,532,853 x 93,758,479 in 54 seconds. (Answer: 7,456,879,327,810,587)

Question 451 ODD ONE OUT

Which of these is the odd one out?

2/2, 4/4, 6/6, 8/8, 10/10, 12/12

Question 452 SINGLE STATE

Can you name, preferably without consulting a map, the only US State which has a single syllable name?

Question 453 CITIES

In which city will you find truth and in which city will you find falsehood?

Question 454 GIRLFRIEND

Bill said to his new girlfriend, 'Is one hug enough?' and she replied, 'Yes.' Why?

BRAIN FLASH: The Herschel family, active in the 18th and 19th centuries, was extraordinarily productive in astronomical discovery. Sir Frederick William Herschel (1738-1822) discovered Uranus in 1781. He also discovered two satellites of Saturn and the rotation of Saturn's rings. His sister, Caroline Lucretia Herschel, discovered eight comets, several nebulae and published a star catalogue, while Sir Frederick William's son, Sir John Frederick William Herschel, discovered 525 nebulae and clusters and in 1848 became President of the Royal Astronomical Society.

Question 455 JUST IN TIME

Find a four-word phrase, meaning just in time, where the last letter of the first word is the same as the first letter of the second word, with this pattern being repeated throughout the phrase.

Question 456 CORRECTION

The equation 123456789 = 100 is obviously wrong. Can you correct it by the addition of just three plus (+) or minus (-) signs between the digits on the left, keeping their order the same?

Question 457 VOWEL TREE

Can you think of a tree, the name of which contains all five vowels?

Question 458 SEQUENCE #18

What is the next number in this sequence?

61, 52, 63, 94, 64, ??

Question 459 CLUED ANAGRAMS

Can you find words meaning: big, kingly, a drink, a hateful look and a composer, which are all anagrams of each other?

Question 460 BLANKS

Can you fill in the blanks in this multiplication?

ABCD x E = FGHI7

The letters represent all the digits bar 7.

Question 461 IN ENGLISH

What do the following words have in common?

Axe, defence, speciality, draught, moult, vice, colour.

Question 462 US STATES

Of the 50 states of the USA, which of them has the most Northerly territory; the most Southerly; the most Easterly and the most Westerly territory?

Question 463 NINES

Using the figures 9999 and as many mathematical symbols as you like, can you make 100?

Question 464 BACK AND FORTH

Forwards, it's heavy, backwards, it's not. What is it?

Question 465 NINE ANAGRAMS

Can you think of a collection of five letters which can make 9 different words, all anagrams of each other?

Question 466 FIVE ANAGRAMS

Things; little things; a newspaper; gives out; to strike. Can you find five five letter anagrams?

Question 467 ABC

'A', 'B' and 'C' are three four letter words. A and B have the same letters in reverse order (like mart and tram). AC is an eight letter word which is a cryptic clue for B. CB is an e letter word and a cryptic clue for A. What are the words?

Question 468 SEQUENCE #19

Which is missing in the following sequence and why?

10, 11, 12, 13, 14, 15, 16, 17, 20, 22, 24, 31, 100, ?, 10000, 1111111111111111.

Question 469 SEPTEMBER 1753

What happened in England between the 3rd and the 13th of September 1753?

Question 470 CRYPTIC ANAGRAMS

A poet steals a girl's meat and fish. Can you write a six-word sentence to this effect which contains five words which are all anagrams of each other?

Question 471 GENERAL INCREASE

What has, in general, increased from 405 to 625 since the 1960s?

Question 472 THINKING

Can you change the word THINK to BRAIN in seven steps, by changing one letter at a time and forming a proper word at each stage?

Question 473 THREE LETTERS

Can you find words which contain the following letter sequences?

XYG, XOP, WKW, YZY

Question 474 SEQUENTIAL TIMES

23 minutes past one, 26 minutes to one ...

What is the next and final item in this sequence?

Question 475 MONKS

What is the collective noun for monks?

Question 476 UNIQUE NUMBER

How is the number 40 unique? (Hint: it is not a mathematical property.)

Question 477 COMMON PLACE NAMES

Apart from being place names. What else do the following have in common?

Salisbury, Newcastle, Liverpool, Derby, Aberdeen.

Question 478 MINUTE HAND

Between now and the same time tomorrow how many times will the minute hand pass the hour hand?

Question 479 ANOTHER UNIQUE NUMBER

Why is this number unique?

8,549,017,632.

Question 480 COMPOSITE

Can you think of a two syllable word, composed of a verb and a noun, the latter seeming to contradict the meaning of the whole?

Question 481 SEQUENCE #20

What number is next in the following sequence?

4, 6, 2, 4, 2, 3, 9, ?

Question 482 EMPHASIS

What is common to the following words?

Produce, import, attribute, rebel, conduct.

Question 483 YORKSHIRE AND SHROPSHIRE

Can you think of two ten letter English place names which each feature the same letter used five times? (The actual letter is not the same in both cases.)

Question 484 PALINDROMIC GREEK

Can you think of an ancient Greek whose name consist of three successive palindromes?

Question 485 ARITHMETICAL SIGN

Using only one arithmetical sign, complete the following equation correctly.

10 10 10 = 9.50

Question 486 DRINK DRIVING

Can you change DRINK to CRASH in seven steps, changing one letter at a time and making correct words all along?

Question 487 CALCULATOR

What 7 digit number can you enter into a calculator, turn the calculator upside-down and the display then shows a word meaning 'pursuits'?

Question 488 TWO LETTERS

Which commonly used, everyday word with a total of eleven letters, contains 2 D's, 2 R's, 2 N's and 2 U's ?

Question 489 CORRESPONDENT

Can you find an anagram of 'Mediterranean Boys Know'?

Question 490 ODD WORD OUT

Pick the odd one out in the following words or phrases:

'Word', 'Noun', 'TLA*', 'Verb', 'Not a sentence'

(Note that TLA stands for Three Letter Acronym)

Question 491 SEQUENCE #21

What is the next number in the following sequence?

2, 5, 5, 4, 5, 6, 3, 7, ?

Question 492 ELEMENTARY

What do the following have in common?

gold, iron, lead, mercury, potassium, silver

Question 493 SINISTER

What is the sinister link between typists and stewardesses?

Question 494 COMMON WORDS

What do these words have in common?

bouquet, charm, kettle, parliament, raft, wedge

Question 495 SEQUENCE #22

What comes next in this sequence?

1, 2, 3, 2, 1, 2, 3, 4, 2, 1, ??

Question 496 SEQUENCE #23

What are the next two terms of the sequence

1, 2, 6, 12, 60, 60, 420, 840, ??, ??

Question 497 MULTI-NATIONAL

What eight-digit number can you enter into a calculator, turn the calculator upside-down and the display then shows two words naming a multi-national company?

Question 498 FAR AWAY

Add two Es to the word FAR to make another English word.

Question 499 COMMON WORDS

What do the following words have in common?

Berate, medallion, scatter, passing, canape

Question 500 INSERTION

Insert one letter somewhere in the middle of the following words to obtain a logical collection.

Coin, peer, lace, bran, jams

SOLUTIONS

1) Isthmus.

2) 6 (each horizontal row has two numbers that are half the other two).

3) 7 (add the numbers top right and top left and divide by three).

4) 6. Number of letters in the days of the week, starting Monday.

5) Oct. For example, triplets, sextuplets, quadruplets and octuplets.

6) 229. The differences between progressive pairs of numbers is 15, 30, 60 and so 120 is added to 109 to give the final number.

7) 125. Successive numbers are obtained by adding 1, 3, 9, 27. The next number in this sequence (the numbers are powers of 3) is 81. 44 + 81 = 125.

8) 104. Successive numbers are obtained by adding 0, 1, 8, 27. The next number in this sequence (the numbers are cubes, i.e. $0^3=0$, $1^3=1$, $2^3=8$, $3^3=27$) is 64. 40 + 64 = 104.

9) Tony. Labour party leaders: Harold Wilson, James Callaghan, Michael Foot, Neil Kinnock, John Smith and Tony Blair.

10) Only Woktu is bogus, the rest are genuine.

11) ALPHA = 27 and OMEGA = 19. (G=0, E=1, L=2, O=3, T=4, P=5, A=6, I=7, H=8, M=9).

12) 7 + 478 + 673 + 9095 = 10253.

13) Conduction.

14) Polyphemus is the one-eyed cyclops, Sleipnir was the eight-legged horse of Wotan, Shelob is the monster spider in the Lord of the Rings (eight legs), The Kraken is a giant ten-tentacled squid and the giant Briareos had 100 arms.

15) 216. The two previous numbers are multiplied together and the result divided by 2. The answer 156 is a justifiable alternative to 216, since the sequence increases each time by successive factorials: 1 (1!), 2 (2!), 6 (3!), 24 (4!), with the next being 120 (5!), giving 36+120 = 156.

16) a) SURGEON; b) ASTRONOMER.

17) 142857 x 3 = 428571.

18) E: Initial letters of One to Eight.

19) 29. The number is reached through the sum of alpha position (A=1, B=2, C=3 etc) first letter plus the square of alpha position for the second letter. Thus T = 20 and C = 3; $20 + 3^2 = 29$.

20) Adieu and Audio.

21)

```
  957
+ 528
 ----
 1485
```

22) Marmoset.

23) Wednesday, sum of alpha position (A=1, B=2, C=3 etc).

24) a) Jasper; b) Myrtle; c) Basil (herb); d) Louis.

25) Noel!

26) Water (H_20).

27) The ages are 25, 4 and 2. These sum to 31, as do 20, 10 and 1 (the product of which is also 200). This is why the census taker needs the extra information. It can be deduced that the number of the house is 31 since this is the only number that requires the census taker to seek further information.

28) Whales. Gaggle and Pod are the appropriate collective nouns in each instance.

29) AND = 498. Each new word adds one to the original value of a letter.

30) Murder. Murder and Pride are the appropriate collective nouns in each instance.

31) 5325 and also -5325. Two negative numbers multiplied together always yield a positive result.

32) Ball.

33) MacBeth called the witches jugging fiends.

34) No. The act of catching a falling object exerts sufficient force to destroy the bridge.

35) 8, 5, 4, 9, 1, 7, 6, 3, 2. The numbers are placed in alphabetical order (eight, five, four, nine, one, seven, six, three and two).

36) Turn switch one on and wait ten minutes. Then turn switch one off, turn switch two on and enter the room. One lamp will be lit, corresponding to switch two. Now feel the other two lamps – the hot bulb will be connected to switch one and the cold one to switch three.

37) DAH. Replace each letter with its alphabetical position and the sums will then make sense.

38) V. All the letters have an 'EE' sound when spoken.

39) G. The letters are the initials of colours. Red and Yellow mixed together give Orange, Blue and Red give Purple and Yellow and Blue give Green.

40) 11. The previous two numbers are added each time to give the next number.

41) SAVIOUR and VARIOUS.

42) 234. The alphabetical position of the first and last letter in each name are multiplied.

43) FEWER. It is not a palindrome (a word that reads the same forwards as backwards).

44) 50p.

45) SPRING, SUMMER, AUTUMN, WINTER.

46) 49. In each name the first Roman numeral minus the last Roman numeral gives the age (C – L = 50; L – V = 45; V – I = 4; L – I = 49).

47) J. (January, February, March, April, May, June).

48) Chloe has 7 sweets and Sam 13.

49) T.S.ELIOT, DRYDEN, MILTON, SHAKESPEARE.

50) Shakespeare. Trinculo in *The Tempest*.

51) They are geological periods, the most recent being: CRETACEOUS followed by JURASSIC, TRIASSIC and CARBONIFEROUS.

52) William Blake, Songs of Experience – The Tyger.

53) Lady Macbeth in Shakespeare's Macbeth from the speech 'Is this a dagger I see before me?'

54) 4. If two consecutive numbers in the first row are added and the result halved, the number below is generated. For example, (35+37)/2 = 36. This gives the answer (5+3)/2 = 4.

55) Neptune 8; Jupiter 16; Uranus 15; Saturn 18. The number of moons orbiting each planet.

56) Mercury 0.2408; Venus 0.6152; Mars 1.881; Pluto 248.5. Planetary years expressed in earth years as the basic unit.

57) Hydrogen 1, Helium 2, Lithium 3, Carbon 6, Oxygen 8 – these being the atomic numbers of the substances.

58) Pluto – Charon; Saturn – Titan; Uranus – Miranda; Mars – Phobos; Jupiter – Io; Neptune – Triton. The planets are matched with one of their moons.

59) Harrison. Rex Harrison played Professor Higgins and Dr Dolittle, while Harrison Ford played Han Solo and Indiana Jones.

60) Pooh in A.A. Milne's 'Winnie the Pooh'.

61) 3.5 pounds.

62) Alice in Lewis Carroll's 'Alice in Wonderland'. (Lewis Carroll was the pseudonym of Charles Lutwidge Dodgson.)

63) 10^{28}.

64) Neuron.

65) 'The Adventures of Sherlock Holmes' by Sir Arthur Conan Doyle, in the story 'The Five Orange Pips'.

66) II. Twentieth century British monarchs Edward VII, George V, Edward VIII, George Vassily Ivanchuk, Elizabeth II.

67) LIFE OF BRIAN – cinematography; CAMBRIAN – geology; ELGIN MARBLES – classical Greek statues; MANUBRIUM – osteology.

68) 20. b1-h8 is 5 moves, b6 to g1 is 4 moves.

69) Hydrogen 1, Carbon 12, Nitrogen 14, Oxygen 16, Helium 4.

70) Falstaff in Shakespeare's 'King Henry IV, Part II'.

71) Lord Byron – English Bards and Scotch Reviewers.

72) 36. The planets are ranked as to their distance from the sun (Jupiter is 5, Mercury is 1 and Pluto 9).

73) Lady Macbeth in Shakespeare's 'Macbeth',

74) 8. The names represent the total number of kings with that name (Richard III, Stephen – only one and Charles II).

75) African studies – NAIROBI; Middle Eastern studies – BAHRAIN; Modern cartoon techniques – DAN BLAIR; Latin American studies – BUENOS AIRES.

76) Number A – 102564; Number B – 410256.

77) Wellington – Waterloo; Cardigan – Balaklava; Caesar – Alesia; Kutuzov – Borodino; Marlborough – Blenheim.

78) A goes with B (5 mins); B comes back (with the light – 10 mins); C goes with D (30 mins); A comes back (31 mins); A goes with B (36 mins).

79) Evolution, Catastrophism, Santa Maria, Argo.

80) 1326. Dates of accession to the throne, averaged out.

81) Titus.

82) The maximum possible is 8. One solution is a4, b6, c8, d2, e7, f1, g3 and h5.

83) Frederick John Perry was a tennis champion. Matthew Perry was the US Naval Commander who opened relations with Japan. Perry Mason was a fictional lawyer, Perry White is editor of the Daily Planet in the Superman series and The Peer and the Peri is the subtitle to the Gilbert and Sullivan opera Iolanthe.

84) 22, 23 and 35. We factor 17710: 2, 5, 7, 11, 23. This is the unique breakdown in the prime factors. Then the only way to get three numbers, each bigger than 19 is 2x11=22; 5x7=35 and 23 left over.

85) Nelson – Aboukir; Themistocles – Salamis; Howard – The Armada; Howe – Ushant; Don John – Lepanto. Naval commanders and their victories.

86) 5 and 17. They are all prime numbers. The answer is 9,699,690.

87) Acacia. The wildebeest is the prime element of the lion's diet as the acacia is for the giraffe.

88) 6. One more than the total number of colours.

89) AARDVARK.

90) Athlete 3.

91) 138, 276. The numbers either increase by 6 or double.

92) Waterloo. The military career of both commanders was finished at the respective battles.

93) 112, 105. The numbers alternately increase by 9 or decrease by 7.

94) No navel. (Adam was created and not born.)

95) X = 44.

96) Item A costs $47, B costs $51. You purchase C for $63 and have $17 change.

97) John.

98) 11 hours.

99) C, A, B, D, E.

100) Mama bear.

101) 32.

102) Staunton £480; barleycorn £400; Lewis £160; Russian £560.

103) 1200 Francs.

104) Total bill £513. The chairman should have paid £156 and the Vice President should have paid £192.

105) Six – the size of the sets is irrelevant!

106) 200 guests, 300 members.

107) Colonel 'B's wife.

108) She distributed the apples 3, 3 and 5 and then pushed all three bags into the remaining one.

109) The set cost £100.50, while the replacement piece cost 50p.

110) Brunnhilde would have been its great aunt and Sleipnir its great uncle.

111) Do you spell your name with a 'V', Mr Wagner?

112) 300,000 kilometres.

113) Albert.

114) Bilbo Baggins – Smaug the Dragon; Frodo Baggins – Shelob the Spider; Hercules – The Lernean Hydra; Captain Nemo – The Giant Squid; Beowulf – Grendel.

115) a = 23, b = 69, c = 200. a + c – b = 154.

116) Wellington – Copenhagen; Alexander the Great – Bucephalus; Caligula – Incitatus; Wotan – Sleipnir; Perseus – Pegasus.

117) a = 12 or 3 (either double or half the above number); b = 7. Therefore (12 + 3) x 7 = 105.

118) Saqqara – The Step Pyramid; Rhodes – The Colossus; Athens – The Parthenon; Moscow – The Kremlin; Washington – The Lincoln Memorial; Olympia – Temple of Zeus.

119) a = 46 (the sequence is the square numbers, but with the double digits reversed: 8 x 8 = 64); b = 45 (the sequence increases alternately by 2 and 10). Therefore 46 – 45 = 1.

120) Rameses II – Kadesh; Antony and Cleopatra – Actium; Hermann – Teutoberger Forest; Leonidas – Thermopylae; Ulysses S Grant – The Wilderness.

121) a fool and his money are soon parted.

122) 364.

123) 260.

124) 38 groats and 7 pfennigs.

125) 19 groats and 88 pfennigs.

126) The sequence is Phobos (Mars), Io (Jupiter), Titan (Saturn), Titania (Neptune) and Charon (Pluto).

127) As Commander Data would put it: it is ‘a pursuit of undomesticated fowl’ (a wild goose chase), since neither planet has any moons.

128) a) Marston Moor (1644) x Naseby (1645) = 2704380; b) Agincourt (1415) + Hastings (1066) = 2481.

129) The twelve labours of Hercules; the nine Muses; the three Graces; the 24 Books of Homer's Iliad.

130) 2.

131) 6.

132) 150,000.

133) 31.

134) One million (1,000 x 1,000).

135) 927.

136) 606 (600 + 6).

137) The answer 'No!' creates a win-win situation for Sir Galahad. If the Guardian proves him wrong by letting him across, he has achieved his goal. If the Guardian says that Sir Galahad's answer is right then he must allow him across the bridge, because he has given the right answer.

138) Pond, lake, sea. H2O is water.

139) A further 22 hours and 30 minutes.

140) White. The bear is sitting on the North Pole which is due North of all other points.

141) Yes.

142) Yes – if the source of the water is on the same level as the city, water will find its own level and can, therefore, run uphill.

143) Picasso – the artist is the odd one out.

144) Shakespeare – CYMBELINE; Marlowe – TAMBERLAINE; Mozart – ZAUBERFLÖTE; Milton – PARADISE LOST.

145) 119.

146) Pour the contents from three into six and return three to its original position.

147) 5049.

148) Yes. If the number of goblins exceeds the number of possible wrinkles then there must be two goblins with the same number.

149) £2,000.

150) Speed is irrelevant. When they meet they are both the same distance from P.

151) They all mean 'two', respectively in Russian, French, German, Italian and Spanish.

152) 10%.

153) KANT, PLATO, ARISTOTLE and WITTGENSTEIN are all fine, but Rubens was a painter.

154) 4 times.

155) EINSTEIN – RELATIVITY; DODGSON (Lewis Carroll) – LOOKING GLASS; GOETHE – FAUST; NEWTON – GRAVITY; GATES – MICROSOFT.

156) He takes the rabbit across, as the cat will not eat the carrots. He returns alone and then takes the cat across. He then returns with the rabbit and takes the carrots across. Finally, he comes back alone to collect the rabbit.

157) AUSTRALIA – CANBERRA; DENMARK – COPENHAGEN; AUSTRIA – VIENNA; S. KOREA – SEOUL; FINLAND – HELSINKI .

158) 3. Shift A to the mid-point beneath H and I, shift G and J to either side of B and C.

159) A, A, B, B.

160) M or 1000.

161) 14 and 12 between 6 and 2; 18 and 10 between 2 and 4; 16 and 8 between 6 and 4.

162) The 5th Indian clockwise or anti-clockwise to the chief.

163) 'Tough', 'Women' and 'Station' show how 'fish' could be justified.

164) On the analogy of 'ghoti': gnash, honest, people, mortgage and friend, the word 'ghoti' might not even be pronounceable.

165) 54.

166) MERCURY, VENUS, EARTH, MARS, JUPITER, SATURN. The large object is the sun.

167) 6 (32 minus 26).

168) The tank regiment.

169) BULL is to COW as STAG is to DOE.

170) 11.

171) The cold tap rate is 600/30=20 litres per minute. The hot tap rate is 600/40=15 litres per minute. The rate of emptying is 600/50=12 litres per minute. Therefore the total amount of water coming in is 35 litres per minute. 12 litres are leaving the bath every minute. So the rate of the bath filling is 23 litres per minute. So 600/23=26.09 mins.

172) Nonsense.

173) Richard = 6 and Charles = 3. The numbers of the English monarchs are added together, thus Richard I, II and III = 6.

174) Casa Rosada – General Galtieri; The Kremlin – Boris Yeltsin; The White House – Bill Clinton; 10 Downing Street – Tony Blair.

175) 30 hours. Team A completes one hyperdrive and three torpedo armings. Team B completes two sets of hyperdrive.

176) Neither of them!

177) 5 miles. If he starts towards the North Pole and continues beyond it in a straight line he continues from north to south without changing course.

178) They filled the 500 gallon container and used that to fill the 300 one. The residue is 200 gallons. Do this twice and you have 400 gallons.

179) 20,000.

180) Surprisingly, the answer is not the intuitive 600 mph but 583.33 mph. For example if the plane travels 100 miles, the outward leg takes 8.57 minutes and the return leg 12 minutes. Total travel time is therefore 20.57 minutes, which equates to an everage speed of 583.33 mph.

181) They exchange horses.

182) 6.

183) His 99th.

184) Hannibal – Elephants; T.S.Eliot – Cats; Hemingway – Big Game; Darwin – Apes.

185) A: 4 in 7; B: 2 in 7; C: 1 in 7.

186) The four possible solutions are:

a) X + I = II. The left hand side is in Roman numerals, while the right hand side is in our number system (i.e. 10 + 1 = 11).

b) Moving a matchstick from the right hand side, and placing it next to the 'V' creates a square root sign. The equation then reads: the square root of +1 = 1.

c) Moving the vertical matchstick from the plus sign to create 'IV' on the right hand side gives: V – I = IV

d) On of the matchsticks from the right hand side of the equation can be used to create a 'not equals to' sign instead of an equals sign.

187) Intaglio.

188) All are collective nouns: Lions, Ravens and Crows respectively.

189) Cheshire – Cat, Whittington – Mayor, Archer – Sherwood, Stilton – Cheese.

190) INDIVISIBILITY or TARAMASALATA.

191) ABSTEMIOUS, FACETIOUS, CAESIOUS.

192) UNNOTICEABLY, SUBCONTINENTAL, UNCOMPLIMENTARY.

193) Make three sets of three and balance any one set against any other. The heavy ball will then be revealed as being in one of these sets or, if they balance, in the set not weighed. Taking the set identified and then repeating the procedure with two individual balls from this set, reveals the heavier ball.

194) Answer to the nearest second = 5 minutes and 27 seconds after 7.00 am.

195) £51. Add up all three prices and divide by 2.

196) The landlord of the Pig and Whistle pub is complaining to a signwriter about a job: 'The spacing is all wrong,' he said. 'There's too much room between Pig and 'and', and 'and' and Whistle'.

197) Yes. This improves your chances of being correct from one in three to two in three.

If this seems confusing, consider the problem as follows: If you do not change your choice, you will only win if your original guess was correct (one chance in three); if you *do* change your choice, you will always win if your original guess was wrong (two chances in three).

For example: Say the million is in 'c'. If you choose 'a', the host *has* to open 'b' (because he knows that 'c' contains the million) and the switch (to 'c') will be a winning move. Similarly, if you choose 'b' the host *has* to open 'a', and again the switch (to 'c') will win. Of course if you choose 'c' and switch then you lose. But the switch wins two times out of three.

198) Battle of Waterloo – 1815; King Charles I executed – 1649; Battle of Hastings – 1066; Foundation of Rome – 753BC.

199) 4. (4 is the 'square' of 2). There is actually an ingenious alternative solution: IL (Roman for 49 – the square of 7).

200) A and B can, the rest cannot.

201) 3651.

202) Bob, where Tom had had 'had', had had 'had had'; 'had had' had had the teacher's approval.

203) 10 pounds.

204) 10 minutes.

205) Long time, no see (Century).

206) October (because of the extra hour) in the Northern hemisphere. March in the Southern hemisphere.

207) 18. The numbers are square numbers in reverse: 4 squared is 16, 5 squared is 25, etc.

9 squared is 81, giving 18 as the answer.

208) SNAIL, SNARL, SNARE, SHARE, SHALE, SHALL, SHELL.

209) Cain.

210) 81. Everybody loses one match except the winner.

211) 30.

212) Brian LARA. The Aral Sea.

213) BACKFIRED, BOLDFACE, OBFUSCATED.

214) Foreign-backed (as in foreign-backed troops).

215) Abhors, almost, biopsy and chintz.

216) The Tokyo Olympics were held in 1964.

217) 196 (rotation 961, swapped digits 169). There is an alternative solution: 100 (since the rotation 001 = 1).

218) 1558. Years when Tudor monarchs came to the throne (Henry VII, Henry VIII, Edward Vassily Ivanchuk, Mary, Elizabeth I).

219) 676.

220) 77. Subsequent numbers are obtained by multiplying together the digits of the previous one (e.g. 7 x 7 = 49; 4 x 9 = 36).

221) do – done, which is an anagram of 'odd one'.

222) A cob is a male swan and the pen is the female.

223) Over one thousand years ago – 28/8/888.

224) The African grey parrot can acquire a substantial vocabulary, is said to recognise colours and shapes and has been described as having the IQ of a two year old.

225) Swans. They are unusual in that they have three collective nouns. Flock on the ground, fleet on the water and flight in the air.

226) 64. (64 squared is 4096 which is also 16 cubed).

227) James Bond (007).

228) 6889.

229) If you make the largest possible number from the digits 6, 1, 7 and 4 and subtract the smallest, you end up back with 6174, i.e. 7641 – 1467 = 6174. If you try this procedure with any four digit number you will, within seven steps, arrive at 6174.

230) Demeter. Neptune and Poseidon are the Roman and Greek gods of the sea. Ceres and Demeter are the same for the Goddess of cultivation.

231) A Scrabble set. Each letter is used once and only once. The 'R' in 'dear' and the 'D' in 'and' are blanks.

232) 13. 13 squared is 169 and 31 squared is 961.

233) 'ough' is pronounced seven different ways.

234) essayasse (from the verb essayer to try).

235) The sentence is palindromic (reads the same forwards as backwards).

236) Uncopyrightables.

237) They are the final digits of successive square numbers (i.e. 1, 4, 9, 16 etc).

238) YHN. The three letter combinations are created by moving across the three rows of a keyboard from left to right.

239) Exe, Wye, Dee, Tees and Severn all eventually end in sea.

240) 41; 27 September 1951 (note that 1992 is a leap year and that 41 x 271 = 11,111).

241) Any point exactly 500 miles south of the equator.
There is actually an ingenious alternative possibility: starting approximately 140 miles north of the South Pole, or starting approximately 1140 miles South of the North Pole.

242) The South Pole or any point within 1,000 miles of the North Pole.

243) Nothing else in the English Language rhymes with them.

244) Tonic Water.

245) 10 minutes later: 1805 = Battle of Trafalgar, 1815 = Battle of Waterloo.

246) a) SS. French numbers = six, sept; b) SD. French days of the week = samedi, dimanche.

247) Pack my box with five dozen liquor jugs.

248) Catherine was born in 1972 and is 28. Note that it is also theoretically possible for Catherine to be 56 but, despite recent advances, 28 is a more common age to become a mother.

249) They each contain three letters which are alphabetically contiguous, e.g. LMN, NOP, DEF etc.

250) An ounce of gold. Gold is measured in troy weight and 1 ounce troy = 31.1035gms. Sugar is measured in avoirdupois weight and 1 ounce avoirdupois = 28.3495gms.

251) 5 (raised to the 5) + 4 (raised to the 5) + 7 (raised to the 5) + 4 (raised to the 5) + 8 (raised to the 5) = 54748.

252) They are anagrams of one two, three four, five six, seven eight, nine ten, eleven twelve.

253) E1GHT. Replace the numbers with Roman numerals as follows: (4=IV, 9=IX, 5=V and 1=I).

254) Queueing (an acceptable spelling according to Chambers).

255) -40 degrees.

256) Two complete revolutions (the width of the note is approximately 2.7 times the diameter of the 5p coin).

257) Just over three feet (actually one foot x Pi).

258) ELEVEN + TWO = TWELVE + ONE. The two sides are anagrams of each other. There is also a remarkable mathematical feature of this equation: 11 + 2 = 12 + 1 works in all bases above 2.

259) If you count the letters, it gives the constant Pi to 15 digits: 3.14159265358979.

260) St John's Wood.

261) The famous Duke of Malborough who commanded the British army during the War of the Spanish succession won his most celebrated victories at Blenheim, Ramillies, Oudenarde and Malplaquet in 1704, 1706, 1708 and 1709.

262) a) 5 minutes; b) 2,000 flies.

263) They all comprise ten different letters of the alphabet.

264) To accentuate the second letter and thus differentiate Iceland from Ireland, especially in Morse Code, where C is dash-dot-dash-dot and R is dot-dash-dot.

265) Neither. They are yellow.

266) Each word contains a word meaning 'nothing', e.g. naught, nil, love and duck.

267) None. The sum of the digits is 45 which is divisible by 3. Any number which has this property will always be divisible by 3.

268) Too wise you are, too wise you be, I see you are too wise for me.

269) The first letter is as far from the end of the alphabet as the last letter is from the start (e.g. xenophobic: x is third from the end, c is third from the beginning).

270) GATE, PATE, PATH, PASH, POSH, POOH, POOR, DOOR.

271) SPARKLING: SPARKING, SPARING, SPRING, SPRIG, PRIG, PIG, PI, I.
STARTLING: STARTING, STARING, STRING, STING, SING, SIN, IN, I.

272) ASPIRATED, SPIRATED, PIRATED, PIRATE, IRATE, RATE, RAT, AT, A.
CLEANSERS, CLEANSER, CLEANSE, CLEANS, CLEAN, LEAN, EAN, AN, A.

273) 1892, when they were 44, the year would be 1936 (= 44 squared). Note that those born in 1980 will be 45 in 2025 (= 45 squared).

274) If the grate be empty put coal on. If the grate be full stop putting coal on.

275) Catherine puts 3 sweets into each of three bags and then puts all three bags into the fourth bag.

276) 2100.

277) September was originally the seventh month, October the eighth, November the ninth and December the tenth. All names refer to Latin numbers.

278) Pea Green; Key Door; Sea Salt; Swans Fleet; Whales Pod; Locusts Swarm; Handel Concerto.

279) Cacophonous.

280) 2 to the power of 64. 2 to the power of 64 minus 1 is the chessboard answer, but Dante writes 'surpass' and so one more is needed.

281) Nine pounds.

282) Two and five respectively. (The question refers to the number of bars or lines used to form digital numbers.)

283) Bookkeeping.

284) In the English language, E is the most frequently used letter, followed by T, A, O etc.

285) Smile becomes Simile.

286) 155. Multiply the two preceding numbers and then add one, e.g. (1 x 2) + 1 = 3, (2 x 3) + 1 = 7 etc.

287) Stop, spot, post, pots, tops, opts.

288) 2000. Times on a 24-hour clock.

289) If you remove the first letter you are left with names of English rivers.

290) Spring, summer, autumn and winter all have six letters. In French printemps (spring) is much longer than été (summer).

291) rot, sort, tours, routes, rouster, courters, trouncers, recounters, intercourse, resurrection.

292) P. The letters are the initials of the planets in order from the sun.

293) Edgehill and Al Alamein, both on 23 October in 1642 and 1942 respectively.

294) 11 days were lost due to the calendar change in 1752.

295) They are all misnomers i.e. the ring-tailed cat is not a cat, the crayfish is not a fish etc.

296) Buckfastleigh.

297) Each is the only number in the language that has the same number of letters as its meaning.

298) All the words are also French words.

299) Two possible answers are: drapes, padres, parsed, rasped, spader, spared and spread or palest, pastel, petals, plates, pleats, septal and staple.

300) BUSH, BASH, BASE, BARE, BORE, GORE.

301) Morse code.

302) 2,000. It is the next number that does not contain an 'e' in its spelling.

303) House numbers for a front door.

304) Beekeeper.

305) All vowels occur only once in forward then reverse order.

306) 10.

307) Senselessness.

308) Stonechat, partridge, nuthatch and crossbill and all birds. Brimstone is a butterfly.

309) Princes.

310) They can all have any vowel put in the middle to make a word e.g. bag, beg, big, bog, bug.

311) Sight-Screen, Catch-Phrase, Watch-Strap.

312) Valuable – Invaluable.

313) There are many possible answers, including A is Monday and B is Thursday.

314) www – World Wide Web.

315) An hourglass – because of all the sand.

316) The resolution not to keep any resolutions.

317) Knightsbridge.

318) 48 years.

319) Replace each 'y' with 'port': 'Oporto is an important port in Portugal which exports port'

320) They are all units of measurement – respectively for horses, typefaces, length and diamonds.

321) Until. Each word starts with the second letter of the previous word.

322) All four representations are perfect squares: 441, 40401, 10404 and 144.

323) They have four letters alphabetically in sequence and together.

324) A letter (different in each case) can be added to make a new word with the same pronounciation: heArd, sCent, styE, reiGn, Hour, Knew, bUy, Wrest.

325) S-N-O-W (The chemical symbols are Sn, O and W).

326) En suite (onze huit).

327) Columbus – America; Marlowe – Tamberlaine; Goethe – Faust; Gutenberg – Bible; da Vinci – Mona Lisa.

328) Only the stupid ones, the rest have flown away.

329) Deified.

330) Semaphore.

331) DUPUYTREN contains 5 consecutive letters in the reverse order that they appear on the typewriter keyboard. The only word to do so.

332) It goes down slightly. The brick (being denser than water) takes up less volume of pool water than the weight of water it displaced when on the lilo.

333) Pascal, Ole (Gunner Solskjaer), Ada, C and Oberon are all computer languages.

334) A couple of feet or so. The third stomach of a ruminant can be known as a bible.

335) 212. They are the temperatures of boiling water on the four scales, Reamur, Celcius, Kelvin and Fahrenheit.

336) A neighbouring farmer lent them a cow, making the total 18. One half is now 9 cows, one third is 6 cows and one ninth 2 cows, making 17 in total. They divided the cattle and then returned the one left over to their neighbour.

337) The men are grandfather, father and son.

338) Alan puts a lock on the chest and sends it to Bill. Bill then puts his own lock on the chest and returns it to Alan. Alan removes his own lock and sends it back. Bill can then undo his own lock and remove the documents.

339) The tip of the mast, as this created the biggest arc in traversing the globe.

340) None. It is now winter.

341) He is playing monopoly.

342) Assassinate – no letters used twice, some 3 or four times, but none twice!

343) 50p. Press the random button. It won't be random and then you can work out the others.

344) Start the timers together. When 4 has run out turn it over (4 mins) When 7 runs out turn that over (7 mins) When 4 has run out again (8 mins) turn over 7 again. Only one minute's worth of sand has gone through and so inverting it allows you to measure the final minute.

345) He is a space-walking astronaut and his glove came off.

346) Brown bread costs 50p and white bread 40p. The first man paid with a 50p piece, the second man used two 20p coins and one 10p coin.

347) The first one. Water freezes at 32 degrees Fahrenheit.

348) Neither – you are over water.

349) 87 – he's looking at the numbers upside down..

350) The letters of his name are the initial letters of the months July to November, leaving seven months unrepresented.

351) He, Her, Hero, and finally, Heroine.

352) The train for Westlea arrives one minute before the train for Eastlea. Therefore there is a nine minute wait for one and only a one minute wait for the other. On average she will end up in Westlea nine times out of ten.

353) Oddly enough, the answer is TYPEWRITER.

354) A discovered check.

355) A=7, E=1, N=6, T=4. Since 7641 minus 1467 = 6174.

356) 12.8 inches (not 14 – the most obvious answer). Imagine the shoe box folded out, draw a straight line between the two points and apply Pythagoras's theorum.

To visualise why 12.8 inches is the right answer, imagine the box is hollow with the ends missing. Now open it out so it is flat and draw a line directly between the two points. The two short sides of the triangle are 10 and 8 inches respectively. By Pythagoras this gives a length of (approximately) 12.8 for the longer side.

357) They are placed in order according to size.

358) It is the sum of money arrived at by having one of each coin (including £5 Golden Jubilee coin).

359) 73 years.

360) [90010 + 85231] x 4 = 700964.

361) 90 minutes. From 12.15 until 1.45 the clock will only strike once. When it strikes just once for the seventh time in a row you know that it must now be 1.45.

362) They are on Bank of England notes: £50, £20, £10 and £5 respectively.

363) Change the first '+' to a '4', i.e. 545+5=550.
Using the line to make the 'equals' sign into 'not equals' is also valid.

364) I am 45 years old. My father is 81, my daughter is 9 and my son is 1.

365) 9 (numbers across the top of a clock face).

366) H=9, P=1, R=0, O=2, C=8, U=3, S=6, T=7, E=5.

367) 200 miles per hour. The axle is travelling at 100 mph. The rim of the wheel is travelling at 100 mph relative to the axle. Speed relative to the ground is therefore 200 mph.

368) Right, rite, write and wright.

369) I and eye, or orc and auk are two possible solutions.

370) Gaol and Jail.

371) 101. They are the numbers which are the same when viewed upside down.

372) They are the positions of the vowels in the alphabet.

373) The second number is the number of letters required to write the first, e.g. ONE (3), TWO (3), THREE (5) etc.

374) The sentence contains ten different pronunciations of the letter 'o'.

375) 1595. Subsequent terms are created by reversing digits of the previous number and adding to the actual number (e.g. 13 + 31 = 44 ... 847 + 748 = 1595).

376) Cleave, Fast (which mean quickly or stationary – as in stuck fast), or Priceless (meaning 'beyond price' or 'no fixed price').

377) The first six multiples of 142,857 use the same digits and in the same sequence, .e.g. 285,714, 428,571, 571,428, 714,825, 857,142.

378) Break and brake; great and grate; steak and stake.

379) The key is the chemical Periodic Table. Element number 35 is Bromine (Br), 33 is Arsenic (As) and 16 is Sulphur (S). Therefore 35 + 33 + 16 = BRASS.

380) 100.

381) When looking at the component lines which combine to create the numbers of a digital clock.

382) 65:E and 00:h. This is the read out on a digital clock when viewed upside down.

383) They are the 100th, 200th, and 300th day of the year respectively.

384) If typed on a conventional typewriter/PC keyboard each letter is adjacent horizontally, vertically or diagonally) to the preceding letter.

385) Best and worst.

386) 12345679 x 9 = 111111111; 12345679 x 18 = 222222222; 12345679 x 27 = 333333333 etc.

387) Raw and war.

388) Number 8. Batsmen 1, 3, 4, 5, 6, 7 are bowled out in the first over; 2, 9, 10, 11 in the second.

389) E and N. First, Second, Third etc.

390) 02.02, 10.02, 11.02, 12.02, 02.22, 10.22, 11.22, 12.22.

391) Chill – chilli and chilly.

392) Ambidextrously.

393) Text messaging.

394) Digital clocks gave identical displays for time, date and year, e.g. 20:02; 20 02; 2002.

395) 1 + 2 + 3 + 4 + 5 + 6 + 7 + (8*9) = 100.

396) Ell, em and en.

397) 5817 x 6 = 34902.

398) Time flies? You cannot! Their flight is too erratic.

399) 19:59:59 to 20:00:00.

400) Atom (A to M).

401) There are more of them (1996 and 1997 are numbers, not years).

402) They all have five letters.

403) Cinq. Count the number of letters in the word and write that number in French for the next word.

404) Crude and Overt (Covert and Rude).

405) c). Although the total volume of air decreases as altitude increases, the **ratio** of all the consituent gases remains the same, therefore the ratio (as opposed to the amount) of oxygen remains the same.

406) The chair of the PM has arms while the ministers' chairs do not.

407) The second group, because all letters in the first group change their form when they go from capital to small letters, whereas all letters in the second group remain the same, only smaller.

408) The number of dots and/or dashes in the Morse Code alphabet.

409) Cash and cache.

410) Drawers.

411) That that is, is. That that is not, is not. Is that it? It is!

412) SPICE, ICE, and IC (one degree Celcius).

413) Tormentor, enticement, underground.

414) Lima and Mali.

415) Billowy (unless readers can find a better one).

416) Ideology and alopecia.

417) Behind the steering wheel of my car, with a taxi in the rear view mirror.

418) N. Capital letters written with three straight lines.

419) 8. Write out each digit. The last letter of each word is the first letter of the subsequent one.

420) It was a sundial.

421) There are 120 such numbers (5 x 4 x 3 x 2 x 1) and the mean number in each position is 5. Therefore the total will be 120 x 55555 = 6666600.

422) Only one term, which is zero. Note that the sequence of products contains the term (x – x), which is zero.

423) Matchstick and Knightsbridge.

424) Withhold.

425) Reign – Re(s)ign.

426) Around; e.g. 'around 20' and 'a round 20'.

427) Inverness-shire.

428) prescribe – proscribe; step – stop.

429)
67 1 43
13 37 61
31 73 7

430) 60.

431) 55 miles per hour, to give a new reading of 14,041.

432) Reserved, re-served.

433) Sanction.

434) 3 x 9 = 27 (Twenty's even!).

435) Guilt – guilty; jealous – jealousy.

436) 277 (mountains over 3,000 feet).

437) Fructidor and Messidor (months in the French revolutionary calendar).

438) Waterfowl. They are collective nouns for wigeons, sheldrakes, bitterns, mallard and pochard.

439) Fast – feast.

440) A year and a half.

441) 8 goes into 'a' and 9 goes into 'b'. Line 'a' contains numbers that have similar pronunciations to common english words, e.g. won, too, for, ate. Line 'b' does not conform to this.

442) Scent – sent, cent.

443) Outgoing and retiring.

444) 6/(1-3/4)). Six divided by a quarter.

445) Around the rim of a £2 coin (quote from Sir Isaac Newton).

446) Poisson – poison.

447) He is the woman's father-in-law.

448) They are the same.

449) Laughter and slaughter.

450) Cupboard and clipboard.

451) 2/2. If you regard them as dates, e.g. 2 February, 4 April etc, then all will fall on the same weekday of any year except 2/2.

452) Maine.

453) Veracity and duplicity.

454) ONE HUG is an anagram of ENOUGH.

455) At the eleventh hour.

456) 123 – 45 – 67 + 89 = 100.

457) Sequoia.

458) 18. Successive square numbers with the digits reversed.

459) Large, regal, lager, glare, Elgar.

460) 8169 x 3 = 24507.

461) They are all spelt differently in the US (ax, defense, specialty, draft, molt, vise, color).

462) Alaska; Hawaii; Alaska and Alaska. (Alaska's Aleutian chain of islands actually crosses the 180 degree meridian and therefore puts Alaska in both the western *and* the eastern hemisphere).

463) 99 + 9/9 = 100.

464) TON.

465) SPEAR, the other words being asper, pares, parse, pears, prase, rapes, reaps and spare.

466) Items, Mites, Times, Emits, Smite.

467) A – Draw; B – Ward; C – Back.

468) 121 is missing. They each represent 16 expressed in bases from 16 down to 1.

469) Those days never existed so nothing happened. At that time the Julian calendar was substituted by the Gregorian calendar and subsequently those days disappeared.

470) Keats takes Kate's skate and steak.

471) The number of lines making up a TV screen picture.

472) Think, thick, trick, track, trait, train, brain.

473) Oxygen, saxophone, awkward, syzygy.

474) A quarter to midnight (digital clock times: 0123, 1234, 2345).

475) An abomination of monks.

476) Forty is the only number with its letters in alphabetical order.

477) They are all ex Prime Ministers: Marquis of Salisbury, Duke of Newcastle, Lord Liverpool, Lord Derby, Lord Aberdeen.

478) 22. (The hour hand goes round twice.)

479) It's in alphabetical order (with 0 = nought; unless you call 0 zero, in which case it's at the end!).

480) Spendthrift.

481) 8. They are the number of letters in the words of the question.

482) Emphasis on the first syllable makes a noun, emphasis on the second makes a verb.

483) Lilleshall (Shropshire) and Nunnington (North Yorkshire).

484) Agamemnon.

485) 10 TO 10 = 9.50 (Time).

486) One solution is drink, drank, frank, flank, flask, flash, clash, crash.

487) 5318804 = hobbies.

488) Underground.

489) Two Brains Raymond Keene.

490) They are all self defining except Verb, e.g. 'Word' is a word. 'Noun' is a noun, 'TLA' is a TLA. 'Not a sentence' is not a sentence. However 'verb' is not a verb.

491) 6. The numbers refer to the numbers of 'bars' lit for each digit from 1 to 8 on a standard digital display. The number for 9 is 6.

492) Their chemical symbols (Au, Fe, Pb, Hg, K, Ag) are NOT abbreviations of their English names.

493) 'Stewardesses' is normally typed with the left hand (hence sinister i.e. left-handed).

494) They are all collective nouns for birds:

a bouquet of pheasants
a charm of finches or hummingbirds
a kettle of hawks
a parliament of owls
a raft of auks, coots or ducks
a wedge of swans or geese

495) 2 (number of characters in Roman numerals I,II,III, IV,V etc)

496) 2520, 2520, the sequence being the least common multiples of 1, 1&2, 1&2&3, 1&2&3&4 etc.

497) 71077345 (Shell Oil)

498) Software (= FAR + TWO ES)

499) They all contain an animal: BeRATe, medalLION, sCATter, pASSing, canAPE

500) Boy's names: Colin, Peter, Lance, Brian, James

CONTRIBUTORS

The authors would like to thank the following who have all made excellent contributions to the Two Brains column over the years.

Special mention should go to:

James Clarke of Woking and Walter Reid of Bangor, Co. Down

who are by far the most frequent contributors to the column. Other regular correspondents include:

Rajiv Bobal, Poole
Christopher Clapham, Exeter
Brian Griffiths, Wantage
Sir Jeremy Hanley KCMG
Melvyn Haynes, Northants
Bob Simpson, Edinburgh

Contributors

Bill Adair, by email
Dr. Johnson F. Ajayi, Southport
Margaret Akmakjian, Cydweli
Mark Ansell, by email
P. Ansell, Hampshire
Barry Banson, Kent
Bill Bardsley, Hove
Jeff Barnes, Middlesex
Roger Barton, by email
A. Bates, Cambridge
Tony Beaulah, Essex
Alison Blenkinsop, Aldershot
Robin Bligh, Surrey
Rob Blyth, Perth
Michael Bond, by email
Stephen Bowen, by email
Keith Boyd, Northampton
Patrick Brady, Tyne and Wear
Jack Britton, Nottingham
Geoff Brown, London
Hugh Brown, Cornwall
P. Browne, Oswestry
Rollo Bruce, Chipping Norton
J.N. Burke, Glasgow
Stephen Burrows, Grantham
Dr. John Burscough, North Lincs

Ruth Camm, Skipton
C. Campbell, Surrey
Patrick Cartright, by email
Charles Clarke, Edinburgh
P. Clements, York
Tim Coleman, Kent
John Collins, Hertfordshire
Gordon Cook, Arbroath
R. Coppull, Chorley
Richard Corkill, Bakewell
Peter Cottee, Bishops Stortford
Alan Cox, Carmarthenshire
J. Crampton, Cheshire
Peter Cunningham, Southend-on-Sea
Robert Dangoor, Mayfair
Colin Davenport, Bucks
Dudley Dennington, Surbiton
Iain Devine, by email
Prof. Nathan Divinsky, Vancouver, Canada
Paul Downham, Cambridge
Billy Downing, Northamptonshire
Paul Dunn, Crowborough
Desmond Dwyer, Birmingham
Paul Dyson, by email
E. Eagling, Andover
Lewis Edge, Burton-upon-Trent
Joyce Egan, Bromley
Nick Elsley, London
David Elston, Edinburgh
Geoffrey Entwistle, Stockport
Arthur Esberger, Telford
Reg Fort, Tewkesbury
Jeffrey Frankland, Cumbria
Hector Fraser, East Yorkshire
Keith Fuget-North, Southampton
Reg Gale, Warwickshire
John Gavin, Cheshire
Alan Gibbs, South Wales
J. Gill, Surrey
Lionel Goldhill, by email
Ian Gordon, Exeter
Richard Green, Winchester
Charles Grene, Somerset
Jack Griffiths, Worthing
Eric Grunwald, by email
David Hall, York
Dan Hallas, Leeds
David Handscomb, Abingdon
David Hannon, Loughton
Eric Hartland, Haverfordwest
Henry Haslam, Taunton
Graham Heald, by email
Rob Heather, by email
Ray Henderson, Co. Down
Jean Hepple, Tyne and Wear
Nicholas Herbert, Dublin
Ian Hinton, Cambridge
Steve Hogg, South Yorkshire
Chris Holman, Middlesex
Derek Holmes, Havant
Dafydd Hughes, by email
R. Hunt, Cornwall
Judith Jackson, Leicester
Amwyn Jones, Llanelli
David Jones, London
John Jordan, Bournemouth
Alan Kendall, Stockton-on-Tees
Des Kite, Warwickshire
A. Kitrick, St Albans

Michael Kindred, Nottingham
Harold Lambert, Cambridge
Janice Lamond, by email
A. Launceston
George Law, by email
Keith Lawrence, Manchester
Andrew Leach, Milan
Su Leavesley, Norwich
David Leibling, by email
John Lethbridge, Oxfordshire
John Lewis, Hertfordshire
Kevin Lowe, Co. Armagh
T. Lowther, Berkhamsted
Vivien Lucas, Derby
Dr. A. Lynch, Potters Bar
John Lynn, Norfolk
C. Machin, York
George Mackay, Ayrshire
A. Malcolm, Guernsey
Dr. E. Mansfield, Surrey
P. Marlow, Crowborough
Stephen McCarron, East Kilbride
Ken McGowan, Dublin
Paul McKenna, by email
Hugh McKinney, by email
Paul Methven, Somerset
Christopher Mitchell, Guildford
Keith Monk, Sevenoaks
Jenine Moodie, by email
R. Morgan, Aberdeen
Prof. Ian Morison, Loughborough
V. Moyses, Banbury
Michael Mullens, by email
Mick Murrihy, Streatham
L. Nagpaul, London
Richard Need, Surrey
Robert Neil, Perth
Jean Newman, Nottingham
Roger Newman, Leicester
Christopher Nethercoat, Somerset
Jack Norfolk, Sudbury
Sean O'Boyle, West Sussex
Bruce Oliver, Hampshire
Terry Owens, Burnopfield
Gary Palmer, South Dakota, USA
Peter Pantelidakis
Jane Parker, by email
Jeremy Parker, Haywards Heath
Nick Parker, Somerset
Anth Pearson, Cumbria
John Perrett, Essex
Daniel Phillips, by email
David Poyner, Essex
Prof. George Pratt, Exeter
David Pritchard, Surrey
Joan Pritchard, Windsor
Ken Proudler, by email
Susan Purcell, Surrey
David Putnam, London
Akef Adib Qusous, Jordan
Stephen Raleigh, London
S. Reich, Salford
Tim Reynolds, Salisbury
David Ribbans, Luton
Daniel Roberts, London
David Robinson, by email
Bill Rogers, Doncaster
Peter Roscoe, Preston
Carol Rosenberg, Baltimore
Alan Ross, Malaga, Spain

Mike Ross, Leeds
Alec Rothwell, Lancashire
Howard Sanders, Oxford
Alan Schofield, North Wales
Anne Senior, Stoke-on-Trent
Ian Service, Cheshire
John Sharples, Cumbria
Michael Sherbourne, London
M. Silvani, Wolverhampton
Paul Silver-Myer, by email
John Smith, Sussex
Martin Snellgrove, by email
Philip Spinks, by email
Robin Spon-Smith, London
Tony Steynor, Derby
Rev. Michael Studdert, Surrey
Chris Suddick, by email
Chris Sutcliffe, Keighley
Brendan Taggart, Switzerland
Len Tapsell, Chester
Ean Taylor, Doncaster
Rod Taylor, Middlesex
Robert Teuton, Cotterell
Anthony Tibbs, Somerset
~~Margot Turnbull, Worcester~~
Gilbert Vernon, London
Alan Wadner, by email
Roc Walker, by email
Martin Wall, by email
Henry Watson, North Yorkshire
Tony Watson, by email
Richard Wells, London
Norman Wenn, Cambridge
W. Whalley, Bognor Regis
Norman Wheatley, Redditch
Jack Whiteley, Spain
S. Wildey, Hertfordshire
Pamela Wilford-Smith, Hertfordshire
Paul Wilson, by email
Gabrielle Williams, King's Lynn
Joyce Williams, Hertfordshire
George Wingfield, Somerset
Jean Winther, by email
George Wood, Stroud
Rev. John Wright, Brighton
Kenneth Wright, Middlesborough
Martin Yates, by email